THE KEY WORK OF SCHOOL BOARDS

A GUIDEBOOK

KATHERYN W. GEMBERLING

CARL W. SMITH

JOSEPH S. VILLANI

"PROFILES OF LEADERSHIP" CHAPTERS
BY BRUCE BUCHANAN

NATIONAL SCHOOL BOARDS ASSOCIATION
ALEXANDRIA, VIRGINIA
2009

COPYRIGHT 2009, NSBA. ALL RIGHTS RESERVED
ISBN: 978-0-88364-309-9
WWW..NSBA.ORG/KEYWORK

TABLE OF CONTENTS

v   FOREWORD

vi   PREFACE

02   CHAPTER 1 SYSTEMS THINKING

10   CHAPTER 2 VISION

16   CHAPTER 3 STANDARDS

22   CHAPTER 4 ASSESSMENT

30   CHAPTER 5 PROFILE OF LEADERSHIP: METROPOLITAN SCHOOL DISTRICT OF WARREN TOWNSHIP

34   CHAPTER 6 ACCOUNTABILITY

40   CHAPTER 7 ALIGNMENT

52   CHAPTER 8 PROFILE OF LEADERSHIP: KENNEWICK SCHOOL DISTRICT

56   CHAPTER 9 CLIMATE AND CULTURE

64   CHAPTER 10 PROFILE OF LEADERSHIP: YORK COUNTY (VA.) SCHOOL DISTRICT

68   CHAPTER 11 COLLABORATION AND COMMUNITY ENGAGEMENT

76   CHAPTER 12 CONTINUOUS IMPROVEMENT

84   CHAPTER 13 PUTTING IT ALL TOGETHER—BECOMING AN INFORMATION AGE BOARD OF EDUCATION

90   CHAPTER 14 PROFILE OF LEADERSHIP: CALVERT COUNTY PUBLIC SCHOOLS

95   REFERENCES AND RESOURCES

96   ACKNOWLEDGEMENTS

97   ABOUT THE AUTHORS

98   ABOUT NSBA…

FOREWORD

Never has public education been more important, and never has it been under such scrutiny. The challenges come at us from all sides: politicians, the media, and the public. And that's why school board members, on the front lines of public education, need to be better trained, more prepared, and deeply engaged in the work being done. The board is responsible for putting in place the proper keystones for students to learn and achieve at the highest level possible. The primary agenda of board members is raising student achievement and engaging the community to attain that goal.

When the National School Boards Association created the Key Work of School Boards in 1999, we strove to create a framework for raising student achievement through community engagement. But much has happened in public education since 1999, and we must move with the times. The No Child Left Behind Act did a lot for and to public education —and board members must be equipped and prepared to meet the challenges that the law and its successors pose for our school districts. Now more than ever, our boards must use data to drive decisions.

Focus has been pulled toward a new set of skills, including technology literacy, global awareness, and real-world practical application. The Key Work of School Boards arms boards with the tools necessary to increase student achievement, not just on core areas, but on those necessary 21st century skills. This guidebook provides information for understanding and implementing the Key Work. It is intended as a support to help school boards understand and achieve the essential elements of their work. The guidebook provides a framework of eight "key" action areas that successful boards have focused their attention on: vision, standards, assessment, accountability, resource alignment, climate, collaboration, and continuous improvement.

NSBA is proud of the work school boards do and the role they play in creating the quality public education system that is fundamental to a strong democratic society. We offer this guidebook as a resource to help boards of education carry out their responsibilities for creating equity and excellence in public education and for leading the community in preparing all students to succeed in a rapidly changing global society.

Anne L. Bryant
Executive Director

PREFACE

THE KEY WORK OF SCHOOL BOARDS: GOVERNANCE TO IMPROVE STUDENT ACHIEVEMENT

The first Key Work guidebook was written in 1999. Why, almost a decade later, are we writing a second edition? Have we changed our key components for board leadership in improving student achievement? Do we need to go in a different direction? The answer to these questions is a resounding no. Then why bother with a new guidebook?

If all we are doing is providing some simple updates, there would be little gain. The second edition is much more than that. This guidebook reflects not only the significant changes in education brought about by new federal and individual state legislation but also the options that evolving technology brings to educational leadership. More important, this guidebook reflects the lessons learned over this past decade working with school districts and school boards who are surviving and thriving in this new era of public accountability.

When we wrote the original Key Work guidebook, each of the authors had recently left careers spent in public education, "growing up" from teacher to principal to district–level senior leaders. In the past decade our focus has shifted to supporting the work of school boards directly through various levels of local boards, and state and national associations. We have learned much about the role and strength of state school boards associations. We also have observed the changing role of school board members.

The passage of the No Child Left Behind Act in 2001 has contributed significantly to these changes; however, it is not solely responsible for them. School board leaders are realizing that the Information Age is bringing access to data for better decision making. We all have better ways to measure quality education. Critical concepts such as return on investment and continuous improvement, once confined to the corporate world, are now part of the discussion at the board tables in school districts all over the country.

This decade has taught us much. One of the best parts of writing this new guidebook has been the opportunity to reflect on what we thought and said 10 years ago and to look at where we see things today. We were struck by how well the eight key components identified in the Key Work had stood the test of time. In fact, some of the components that were introduced as a new way of focusing the work of school boards are now fundamental to how many boards function. Many of the challenges raised in the Key Work now appear to be predictions of the changes that have come to pass. Ideas that required explanation and advocacy in contrast to practices and policies in place at the time now are accepted components (prime example—disaggregated data).

Most state school boards associations have realigned their training to focus on helping boards govern to increase student achievement. Many of them use the "Key Work" framework as the basis for their board development activities, and others have developed their own admirable frameworks for governance for student achievement. We encourage you to participate actively in the opportunities that your state association makes available to you. Sharing your thinking, your experience, and your questions with colleagues in your state or region is an excellent strategy for expanding and deepening your understanding of why and how you must focus on student achievement if you are going to be a successful board member.

Everywhere, student results are now the fundamental measure of a school district's efficacy and that of its individual schools. No longer can low-achieving schools and districts maintain an illusion of success. Success is measured not only in attaining standards but also by demonstrating improvement. In addition, the analysis of student achievement by various subgroup populations has required the focus on closing learning gaps. In the struggles to reach new standards we have encountered both victory and defeat. Paying attention to what works and what doesn't is critical to determining the future direction for attaining quality education for all students.

It is in keeping with the constant challenge to improve student achievement that we offer this second guidebook. Do we have all the answers? We do not. Do we have perspectives worth sharing based on the experiences of the past decade? We believe we do.

In addition to the overall rewriting of the book, we have included new materials that we hope will make it more useful. We have added a chapter at the end of the book to help boards get started in pulling all the components together. In particular, this chapter addresses understanding the need for a strong information foundation that provides feedback data at all levels—classroom, school, district, school board. High-performing districts use data to inform their decisions at all levels. The technology options and supports available to school districts have vastly increased since the original publication.

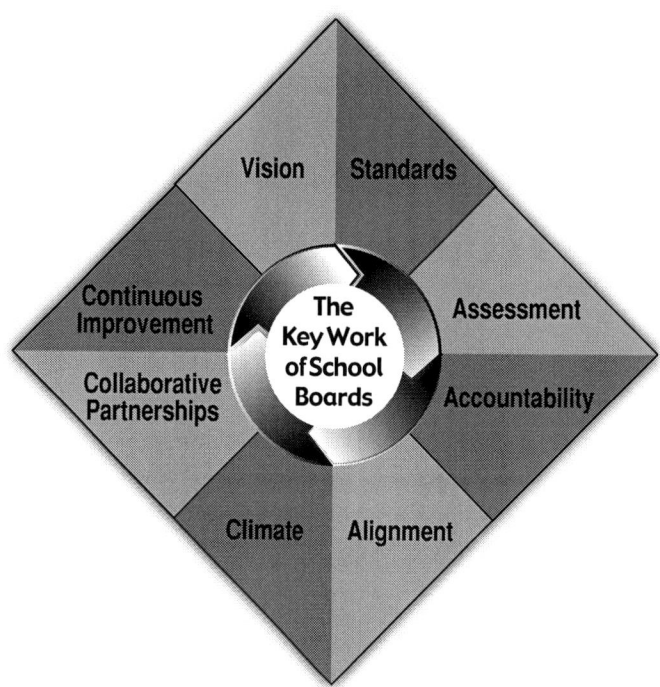

Interspersed throughout this book are four "Profiles of Leadership" that illuminate how several school districts have used the concepts in The Key Work to achieve positive results for student achievement. The districts profiled were recommended by their state associations as examples of what hard work, collaborative action, and strong leadership can accomplish when the board and superintendent work together in a systematic way—like the system that is the Key Work. The stories are powerful reminders of the difference that leadership makes, the leadership that is the call of every school board member.

We will keep the Key Work information current by maintaining updates and school board best practices on the NSBA website (www.NSBA.org/keywork). School board members are encouraged to share their experiences of both what worked as well as what didn't. We can all learn from not only our own experiences but also the experiences of others.

In spite of the changes, some things remain the same. The eight fundamental components of the Key Work of school boards are the same—Vision, Standards, Assessment, Accountability, Alignment, Collaboration, Climate, and Continuous Improvement.

The better these eight key areas are integrated into a process, the better the student achievement results will be. School boards that understand and practice these components, not as separate parts but as parts of the whole, can improve student achievement and board effectiveness. The structure of the original guidebook is maintained to enable board members to self-assess, reflect, and take action. The guidebook is designed to allow board members to work on different areas in whatever order meets the needs of the reader. There are questions to help guide understanding and application.

Finally, we have continued our original approach to making this guidebook easy to use. The format consistency should allow readers to find what they need from chapter to chapter. The relatively informal writing style is intended to engage the reader quickly. The guidebook can be used and reused in many different ways by board members. Read and reread the guidebook. Write in it. Copy and reuse individual pages. Highlight passages or sections. We would love it if your copy becomes so dog-eared with use that it resembles your mother's favorite cookbook.

Our purpose in writing the second guidebook is the same as the first—to help school boards improve student achievement through effective governance. The intent of this book is to give you a framework for thinking about your work as a school board member. The challenges facing school boards and public education have never been greater. Unwavering commitment will be required to meet these challenges. If this guidebook can help move that commitment into practices and policies that produce positive results for students, we will have succeeded.

1. SYSTEMS THINKING

The key work of school boards is to improve student achievement and increase community engagement to promote student achievement. As local boards face the challenges of providing effective governance, they are using their time and energy to focus on these twin imperatives. It is no longer either possible or credible for boards of education to serve as passive reviewers and judges of the work of others. This oversight role, assigned to local boards during the early years of the past century to ensure clean government, has changed even as times have changed. Education has become more and more central to our future as a society and our ability to compete in the global marketplace.

The central role of education in personal, social, and economic success has created a new sense of urgency and a growing realization that the knowledge and conceptual understanding expected of college-bound students is now the goal for all students. At the same time, the technological revolution, symbolized by the personal computer and the Internet, is fundamentally changing how we think, work, communicate, and learn. In the 21st century, for example, learning how to work collaboratively with others rather than in competition requires students to think and behave differently. In turn, schools must employ significantly different strategies for teaching and organizing instruction.

Local boards of education are no longer merely overseers of school systems; they are leaders of public education in their states and communities. They are charged with the responsibility to create the conditions within their school districts that enable students to meet rigorous knowledge and performance standards.

Creating optimal conditions for teaching and learning is a formidable challenge. It requires that boards understand issues deeply, align resources, and foster a culture within the system that supports and rewards the work of principals, teachers, and students in improving student achievement. It means that boards take responsibility for results even as they also hold others in the school district accountable. It means that boards articulate the educational mission of the district and garner the public support and resources needed to achieve that mission.

To help local boards carry out their work, the National School Boards Association has developed a framework called the Key Work of School Boards. This framework outlines eight key areas that boards need to focus on:

- Vision
- Standards
- Assessment
- Accountability
- Alignment
- Climate and Culture
- Collaborative Relationships / Community Engagement
- Continuous Improvement.

The Key Work of School Boards provides a framework for planning and acting, a framework based on systems thinking. Several of these same concepts drawn from systems thinking are used regularly to identify, assess, and benchmark quality organizations in business, industry, education, and government.

The Key Work of School Boards is a framework that can help school boards provide the leadership through governance that will create the conditions under which excellent teaching and accelerated student learning can take place. It is based on the premise that excellence in the classroom begins with excellence in the boardroom. Through NSBA's Key Work website (www.nsba.org/keywork) and through state school board associations, every board member has access to useful questions, practical strategies, and resources for implementing the key work.

The rest of this chapter provides a brief explanation of each of the key actions and the role it plays in empowering local boards to create quality, results-driven school

CHAPTER 1

systems. As you read, keep in mind that "systems thinking" means just that. The actions do not represent a "laundry list" of items for boards to check off one by one; in fact, the opposite is true. To be a systems thinker is to realize that the whole, not its parts, makes the difference; these key actions are both linking and inter-weaving. To underscore this point, Peter Senge (*The Fifth Discipline*) observes that it is impossible to cut an elephant in half and get two smaller elephants.

VISION AND MISSION

Vision is not about what we are, but about what we want to be. Vision captures a critical dimension of dynamic systems. For school boards, it is about where we are going and what kind of school systems we are trying to create. A positive vision is future-focused and seeks to shape events rather than simply let them happen. In this new century, we hear more and more calls for visionary leaders who are willing to take risks and who call us to sacrifice to achieve larger purposes. In the same way, public education needs visionary school boards that can speak forcefully about the integral role of public school in our democratic system and engage the community in support of excellent schools and robust programs for all children.

Our history as a nation is replete with examples of powerful visions that continue to shape our thinking and actions. The Declaration of Independence is perhaps our most famous example of a powerful and positive vision statement. When the Declaration was penned in 1776, the notion that all men are created equal was itself revolutionary, for it envisioned a social state that did not exist anywhere in the world. We have spent the last 232 years struggling with what that means. Witness the struggle to ensure women the right to vote, and the civil rights movement that began with the Civil War and accelerated in the 1960s and continues to this day. Witness Martin Luther King's "I Have a Dream" speech that articulated a powerful vision of a color blind society in which individuals would be judged not by the color of their skin but by the content of their character. John F. Kennedy's vision of space exploration—landing a man on the moon, and bringing him back to earth safely—captured the imagination of the American people. It spawned an era of space exploration that simply could not have been imagined 50 years ago except as science fiction. In more modest as well as in these grander contexts, vision is a critical dimension of effective enterprises.

Positive and inspiring visions require the widespread involvement of those whose lives will be influenced and shaped by the vision. Powerful visions are the product of endless hours of discussion and dialogue among key stakeholders. Not too many years ago, boards were advised to go behind closed doors, hammer out a vision and mission for the school district, and submit it to the community for reaction and review. Today we know better. We know that, without involvement, there is unlikely to be much commitment on the part of those upon whom we must rely to achieve it. Compliance and commitment represent two very different levels of engagement. It is a process that Joel Barker calls building the "vision community."

Closely related to vision is mission. At one level, the mission of an organization is what it is created to do. In an effective organization, the mission statement also captures and reflects the core values and beliefs that guide the organization and its members in pursuit of stated aims and goals. Here is one example of a mission statement developed by a school district under the leadership of its elected board: "To shape the future, one child at a time, through a community partnership dedicated to excellence in teaching and learning." Often core values and beliefs and the flavor of the vision are woven into the mission statement. Another important feature of a powerful mission statement is that it is short, succinct, and memorable.

STANDARDS

Another component of a systems approach is the establishment of standards for performance. This is as important for school systems as it is for other enterprises. In systems thinking, major emphasis is given both to quality of performance and to product. In order to know whether we are performing in accordance with expectations, we need to establish specific standards. Those standards need to be tied in realistic ways to the expectations of the community and, just as importantly, to our understanding about what knowledge and skills will be needed by future generations as they respond to the challenges of a rapidly changing social and economic landscape.

All states have established curriculum content and student performance standards for public school students. Boards must consider how these standards affect their decisions. Secondly, many states are implementing new graduation requirements that include satisfactory performance on "high stakes" exit examinations. Local boards need to understand what these tests will require, how they are linked to state-established performance standards, and what the impact will be on students who do not pass.

When board members understand what standards already are in place and how they affect students, teachers, and the community, they can incorporate those standards into district-level standards. These district standards will need to be broadly focused to include not only academic knowledge but also the social and personal skills that students will need as detailed in the Partnership for 21st Century Skills (www.21stcenturyskills.org).

One way that organizations establish quality performance standards is through benchmarking. Benchmarking involves finding and analyzing "best practices" with respect to standards and then developing standards that meet or exceed those benchmarks. For example, if system leaders want to establish mathematics standards for students at each grade level, a critical step would be to identify a district or districts (or national association) that have established mathematics standards and produced outstanding results. This "exemplary" work becomes the starting point for the standards-setting process in the local district. Benchmarking helps the board by giving it a base for action and avoids reinventing the proverbial wheel. Today, the Internet provides an invaluable resource for finding out what others are doing to improve student achievement and building on their work. (NSBA's Key Work website—www.nsba.org/keywork—provides a shortcut for finding out about successful practices to support benchmarking.) Benchmarking is a helpful tool to promote continuous improvement and is the responsibility of the superintendent and staff.

Establishing standards is one of the board's most important responsibilities. Once standards are in place, the superintendent, working with principals, teachers, and others, is responsible for developing the curricula and identifying and using instructional strategies that will enable students to meet those standards.

ASSESSMENT

Promoting outstanding student performance based on clearly delineated standards is central to the key work of school boards. The next step is to determine how well students are doing in meeting those standards. Effective organizations emphasize assessment for two major reasons.

The first reason is that school boards need information in order to make decisions, not only about how well they are doing, but also about what may be needed in order to ensure that system goals for student achievement will be met. Without that kind of information, boards can end up making decisions that are based on conventional wisdom, hunches, and what worked in the past. Margaret Wheatley, a student of effective organizations, argues that information informs and forms both the individual and the organization.

Secondly, having accurate information about how well students are doing creates opportunities for the school system to focus on continuous improvement. When school boards have accurate information in usable formats, they have a powerful tool to ensure that the superintendent and staff are using that information to improve the delivery of services. When teachers have access to reliable data about how students are doing, those data inform and empower their work with students. They are able to make instructional decisions with far greater precision and effect.

Today, a growing number of Web-based organizations are providing school systems with data storage and analysis systems at very reasonable prices. These services give smaller school districts access to information and data analysis tools in formats geared to the needs of teachers, school administrators, superintendents, and boards of education. Gone are the days when only large, wealthy school districts could afford to purchase and maintain sophisticated data storage and analyses systems. For a few dollars per student, the same capacity is now available to school systems whether they have 500 or 50,000 students. Several state school board associations are partnering with service providers to make such services readily available to school systems. Check with your state association for services available in your state.

The goal is to use this information as feedback and a guide. When Peter Senge refers to the "learning organization," he is talking not about schools or school systems but about organizations that are so attuned to their environments that they constantly receive information about how well they are accomplishing their missions and use that information to survive and thrive in changing circumstances.

ACCOUNTABILITY

Increasingly, local school districts are held accountable for how students perform on a variety of assessment measures. Local school boards, similarly, are held accountable for student performance. Fifty years ago, most school boards did not pay much attention to student achievement, and they were not expected to. Performance of students was the responsibility of the superintendent and staff; students were routinely tested and placed in programs (sometimes called tracks) that would enable them to be successful. School boards were oversight bodies that hired the superintendent and ensured that the management of the school district was efficient and effective.

This demarcation of roles worked reasonably well in the Industrial Age, but does not work in the Information Age. A half century ago, it was acceptable to prepare 25 percent of public school students for college and the rest for jobs in factories, the world of business and commerce, and agriculture. Now, successful workers in all fields need the same knowledge and competencies formerly reserved for the college preparatory students. Other factors, including the civil rights movement and the continuing quest for equity that it spawned, increased pressure on school boards and school systems to educate all children at high levels. These fundamental changes in society and the workplace forced a redefinition of the educational requirements for students graduating from high school and posed new challenges for boards of education.

In the past 20 years, increasingly rigorous graduation requirements and performance standards have turned the spotlight on accountability and those who lead. One result is that school boards are called upon to take responsibility for creating the conditions for excellent teaching and learning, and to be as accountable as the superintendent and staff. This means reporting to state authorities and to the community about how well students are doing and what actions are being taken to address perceived deficiencies. It also means taking steps through governance to keep their commitments to the state and community.

Accountability is not unique to schools, of course; other organizations have their own accountability imperatives. In business, it is the bottom line. In manufacturing, it is the quantity and quality of production. In the public sector, it is how well services are being provided. In education, it is student achievement.

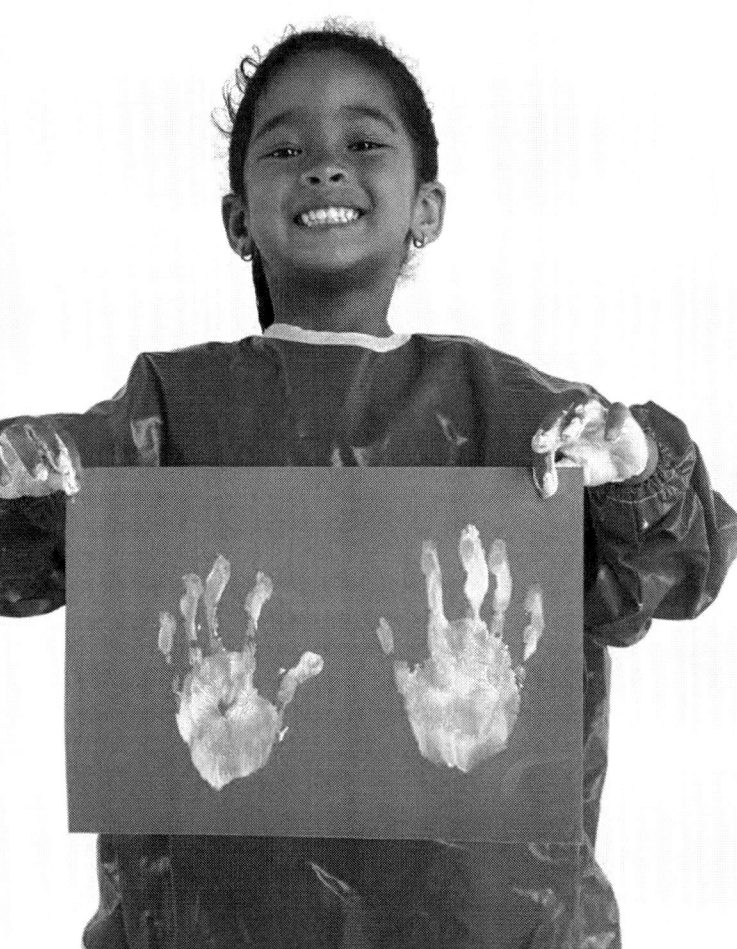

Effective school boards take accountability very seriously, and they dedicate themselves to being responsible stewards and leaders of public education. They mitigate the critics of public education with solid performance results and discernable actions to correct deficiencies.

ALIGNMENT

Alignment is another key component of a systems approach to school board leadership. A critical role of the board is to establish quality standards and system priorities focused on enhancing student achievement. But if the work of the board stops there, it will not be enough. The board is responsible for creating the conditions under which excellent teaching and student learning will take place. Effective system leaders understand that standards will not be met nor priorities achieved unless resources and support are in place to get the job done. Procuring those resources either through the budgetary process or by reallocating existing funds is the first step.

The next critical step is to direct those resources to achieve the system's standards and priorities. Without such deliberate attention to alignment, even the best systems are susceptible to organizational drift. Alignment usually begins with the budget-setting process, but it does not stop there. The school system's budget, approved and adopted by the board, is the key instrument by which the board promotes alignment. Effective boards ask many questions during the budget-setting process, but they also establish in advance expectations for the allocation of scarce resources. If the board has decided that improving reading performance in the early years is a priority, it must make sure that sufficient resources are provided for staff to achieve that goal. Sometimes that means eliminating programs and initiatives that are less important or have not lived up to expectations; sometimes it means convincing the community or other funding agency that additional resources are critically needed.

Alignment, though, is not confined to resources. Some of the most important aspects of alignment have as much to do with mental models, established ways of thinking and acting that get in the way of real progress, as they do with procuring needed resources. For example, the board may establish a priority that calls for all students to master complex mathematical concepts needed for college and the workplace, but if only 45 percent of students take mathematics courses beyond Algebra I, the system is not aligned. The board must play a pivotal role in examining prevailing practices and challenging those that do not support progress toward system goals. This means asking the right questions, requiring data in usable formats, and challenging prevailing aspects of the school system's culture and operating norms.

CLIMATE AND CULTURE

Climate is a key aspect of system culture. Terrance Deal describes culture as "the way we do things around here." Climate is a byproduct of culture and is dependent on it. Leading-edge organizations are very conscious of climate because of its powerful effect on behavior. In one organization, a bell rings every time a major initiative experiences a significant problem. The ringing of the bell reminds everyone that confronting difficulties and solving problems are fundamental to creating new products and more effective ways of operating. What is celebrated is not failure but the human spirit of adventure. In such a climate, individuals are empowered to act boldly and think "outside the box."

Effective school boards give priority to climate as well, because it factors importantly in what students and teachers are able to accomplish. Climate also is a critical determinant of how parents and others in the community view schools. For example, if the principal and faculty of a school believe that parents should be seen but not heard, then parents who express concerns, make suggestions for improvement, or question their child's progress will be viewed with suspicion. They may be labeled as troublemakers and their voices discounted. In fact, in too many schools, parents are told implicitly and sometimes explicitly that school matters belong to the professionals and that the role of parents is to make sure their children are in school and prepared to do what they are asked to do. That way of thinking and acting alienates parents. When schools subsequently come under fire, many of these parents join the barrage.

School boards need to pay attention to climate and culture and take steps to assure that the values espoused by the school system are in fact driving and shaping the climate of schools. Most school systems say that they value parents as partners but the climates of individual schools do not always reflect that value. School systems often proclaim that all children can be successful learners, but the climate of some schools may give children a very different, less inclusive impression. When that happens, many students' feelings of competence and self-worth suffer, and with them, their ability to perform.

School boards that understand the powerful effect that climate has on the behavior and performance of teachers and students, as well as on the perceptions of the community, pay attention to the human dimension of the organization. They articulate values such as respect for others, civility, integrity, and inclusion. They model the behavior they expect from others.

COLLABORATIVE RELATIONSHIPS

Relationships are a critical dimension of effective organizations. That is one reason why students who graduate from high school today need to know how to work with others in team situations. Not too many years ago, the dominant metaphor of success for most Americans was competition. We expressed that metaphor in many ways: "to the victor belong the spoils"; "paddle your own canoe"; "survival of the fittest." Today, we all recognize that competition is still important, but it is not competition among individuals so much as it competition among teams. We know that when individuals work together effectively, the product of their efforts almost always will be superior to the efforts of any single individual. It is a principle we have known for some time; most breakthrough research is the product of team efforts, not individual performance.

The quality of relationships in an organization will largely determine how well that organization produces. Helping to create the conditions that make it possible for teachers to teach well and students to perform not only excellently but also collaboratively is one of challenges of school boards. School boards must have an accurate gauge of the quality of relationships at all levels of the system. In addition, they must be prepared to take affirmative action to promote better relationships where improvement is needed. Finally, they must commit to fostering long-term collaborative relationships, inside and outside the school system.

The board should foster good relations with stakeholders such as the business and political leaders in the community. Sometimes these individuals are perceived as being disinterested in school governance issues or as resistant to the financial and political implications of board actions to improve schools. But many successful school boards have demonstrated that establishing positive relationships with these constituents can create productive partnerships for student success as well as increase their willingness to make political and financial decisions favorable to schools.

Collaboration occurs when people come together and contribute to the solution to a problem or to the creation of new and better ways of achieving desired results. Collaboration is based on trust and mutual respect. It can be encouraged but it cannot be legislated. It means paying attention to teacher and students working conditions and seeking practical ways to improve those conditions. Working conditions are important, but even more important is the way people are treated in schools and by schools. It includes taking the initiative to keep political leaders informed about school successes and shortcomings and giving them recognition when they support the school system's vision for student achievement. It means earnestly seeking advice from business leaders about what students need to know and do to be successful in the workplace.

Boards who understand systems thinking know that promoting collaboration and cooperation requires bringing teachers, parents, students, and community members into the decision-making process. It is hard but important work. It is work that boards must be willing to do if improving student achievement is the goal. The network of collaboration must include students, parents, the business community, higher education, community leaders, in short all those who have a stake in promoting excellent public schools.

CONTINUOUS IMPROVEMENT

Continuous improvement is perhaps the single orientation that most clearly defines the effective organization in the 21st century. Continuous improvement is about paying attention to the quality of what we do. As one continuous improvement advocate expressed it, the goal is not to be 10 percent better in any one area of the operation, it is to be 1 percent better in 10 areas of the operation. The Japanese have a word for continuous improvement: *kaizen*. It means taking whatever the product or process is and making it better. It is a way of thinking and acting that is never satisfied with the status quo; it is an objective that is never accomplished.

Boards that believe in continuous improvement ask probing questions about existing practices, not as a mean of micromanaging but to promote improved practices. Their questions are not hostile but affirming. The board can use questions to encourage the superintendent and staff to develop the habit of continuously seeking ways to improve existing operations and results.

Effective organizations adopt a customer focus. For many educators, the notion of "customer" applied to students, parents, and others is alien and offensive. It has an air of commercialism that is contrary to the educators' world view. Moreover, they are right to be skeptical of this terminology unless it is put in context. Parents and students are not merely consumers where schools are concerned. They are citizens first and the very reasons that schools exist. They have a stake in the schools and a responsibility to support them and also to appreciate the important role they play in the quality of community life. Public schools are bedrock to our democratic system and their efficacy and reputation often determines whether individuals and businesses will choose to locate in one community as opposed to another.

In this context, however, customer focus is not used in the retail sense of that term. Here it means understanding what we do and for whom. W. Edwards Deming, one of the architects of quality management, teaches that everyone in the organization is a customer—and has customers. (For extensive information on Deming's ideas, see his website at www.deming.org.) The central questions for each individual are these: Whom do I serve and who serves me? Answering this question brings focus and purpose to the work we do.

In school systems, many people are doing many things, carrying out endless daily routines, without ever consciously considering how what they do contributes to achieving the district's mission and goals. Bus drivers need to understand, for example, that merely transporting students is not their job. Their real challenge is to transport students in a way that helps them arrive at school ready to learn, not frustrated and anxious. The third-grade teacher serves the fourth-grade teacher by preparing her students to be successful in the next grade, and so forth.

What is true for bus drivers and classroom teachers also is true for school district leaders. School boards must learn to be customer-focused, to understand whom they serve and who serves them. Doing so builds collaborative relationships and fosters a climate where high achievement is valued and celebrated.

THE WHOLE AND ITS PARTS

Governing with a systems perspective means understanding not only that the whole is greater than the sum of its parts, but also that each of the parts is essential. In the chapters that follow, each of these key concepts is explored in greater depth with examples and suggested strategies that boards can use to bring systems thinking into their own school districts and make it central to decision making. As you read through these chapters, keep in mind that effective governance flows from understanding and paying attention to all of these elements of the Key Work. Strive to become a board member who, like a well-trained athlete, exercises all of your major governance muscles and joints in order to put it all together in your leadership for student achievement.

2. VISION

Every system of organizational leadership begins with a clear vision of what the organization wants to achieve. The organization's vision is what it hopes to become, the ideal tomorrow it strives to create today. The more clearly that people within the organization can see this vision and describe it to others, the more compelling the vision becomes. People in leadership positions cannot be everywhere in the organization; leadership must rely on a shared vision to permeate the organization and direct day-to-day behaviors and activities towards its goals. An explicit vision, developed and embraced by everyone with a stake in the outcome, guides and shapes an organization because of its power to motivate, unify, and direct individual purposes and behaviors to achieve common goals. The vision becomes the guiding principle that directs the actions of every person with a stake in achieving it. A powerful vision is an internal and intrinsic motivator that evokes leadership behavior throughout the organization.

Developing a shared vision for student achievement that reflects the common values and core beliefs of a school community is the starting point for a school board and its focus on student achievement. This shared vision is the kernel of the mission and goals that not only directs the board's and the staff's actions but also gains the commitment of the entire community to improving achievement for all students. Engaging the entire community in creating the vision generates support for getting the resources—both financial and human capital—necessary to make it a reality.

THE VALUE OF VISION

Building a shared vision requires that you first are able to agree upon your core values and beliefs. In *The Fifth Discipline Fieldbook*, Peter Senge writes, "Values describe how we intend to operate, on a day-to-day basis, as we pursue our vision." Knowing what you really value, individually and collectively, guides your aspirations and your mission as a district. It also guides your behavior.

Your vision should inspire, look ahead, and lead. In the same way that it makes more sense to steer a car by looking through the windshield instead of the rear-view mirror, school district leadership serves best with a forward-looking vision. What do you know about 21st century demands on students? What does your community aspire to become? What are the global challenges that your students and your community face? Do you recognize what you do not know? Do you comprehend the warp speed at which our world is changing? Coming to grips with these questions will help you in your struggle to create a vision that serves as a roadmap to the future.

Neil Postman writes in the opening sentence of *The Disappearance of Childhood*, "Children are the living messages we send to a time we will not see." A well-developed and clearly articulated vision for your school system can help you see a bit further into the horizon. Defining your vision is taking charge of your destiny. For school districts, that destiny must be improving achievement for all students. A vision with anything less than student achievement as the top priority cannot fulfill the core mission of public education, to make those "living messages" as coherent and well-prepared as they can be.

CREATING A VISION

Vision becomes reality through the daily actions of everyone in the organization. In a school district, "everyone" includes employees, parents, community advocates, businesses, government agencies, and higher education. Engaging the total community makes the vision more likely to be accepted and encourages the behaviors necessary to achieve the vision. As a board of education, it is your responsibility to work with the community to develop student achievement as the top priority.

Achieving such total commitment requires multiple steps. First, gather input from the stakeholders in order to identify their core beliefs and common values. Once those

CHAPTER 2

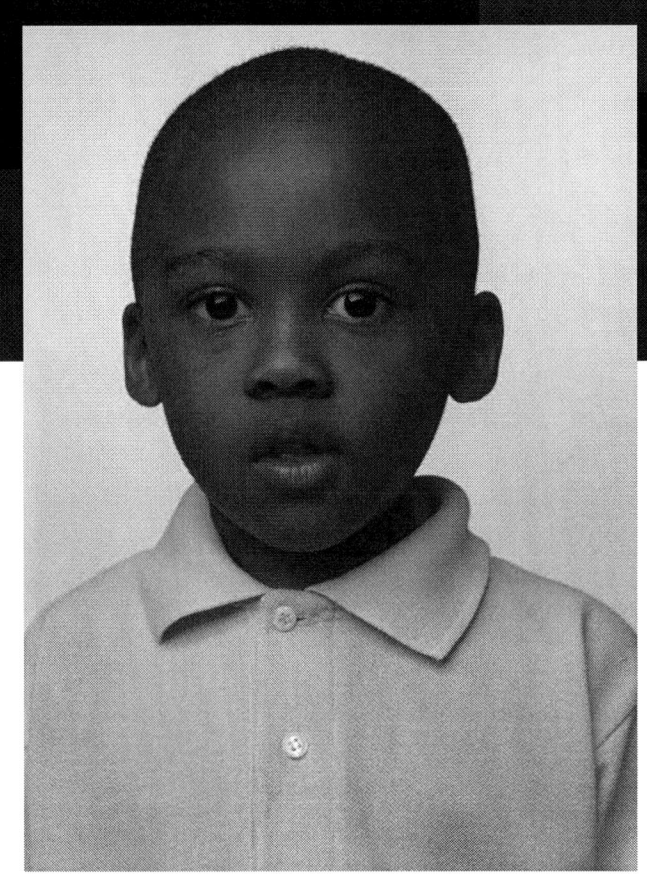

values are delineated, you need a process for drafting a vision statement. After the draft statement is written, you must test the vision. Seek feedback from the stakeholders to ensure that the statement reflects core beliefs and that the vision inspires commitment to student achievement as the highest priority. When the vision statement is complete, the dissemination process begins.

Communication of the vision to the entire community is essential. It is important that you as board members can articulate the main points of the vision. You should articulate these core points at every opportunity when you are together and when you are out in the community. By constantly repeating, reinforcing, and embracing these main components, you will develop the constancy of purpose needed to sustain your vision.

Constancy of purpose will guide your leadership team. Achieving the vision takes time and persistence. The staff members who work on a daily basis to achieve the district's vision need to recognize that this is not a "vision *du jour*," to be changed on a whim. Knowing that your board is committed to investing the time necessary to achieve the vision will motivate staff to persist, to commit themselves to working as hard and as long as necessary to be successful. Your constancy of purpose and commitment to a long-term change in your district gives staff the encouragement to try new ideas that may need time to become successful. Long-term results require long-range thinking and commitment.

The language of your vision statement matters—a lot. Some of the best examples of vision statements in American history are simple, concise, and memorable:

- "We hold these truths to be self-evident, that all men are created equal, that they are endowed by their Creator with certain unalienable Rights, that among these are Life, Liberty and the pursuit of Happiness."
  Thomas Jefferson, 1776

- "I believe that this nation should commit itself to achieving the goal, before this decade is out, of landing a man on the Moon and returning him safely to the Earth."
  John F. Kennedy, 1961

- "I have a dream that my four little children will one day live in a nation where they will not be judged by the color of their skin but by the content of their character."
  Dr. Martin Luther King, Jr., 1963

Each of these remarkable statements created a vision and *ignited a passion* to achieve it. These were not slogans. These statements were powerful tools for creating change because of the elegant simplicity of their language and the compelling complexity of their view of the future. They motivated organizational behaviors in ways their authors could not know. Each carved out a bold leadership challenge and described what achieving that challenge would look like. All three are visions that changed the history of our nation.

Below are some examples of school district visions that may help you in your own district, not because they are perfect but because they are good examples of how others

EXAMPLES OF VISION STATEMENTS

Listed below are several vision statements from school districts across the country. These examples may help clarify your thinking about what statement you want to make about the vision for student achievement in your district.

"A high-quality education is the fundamental right of every child. All children will receive the respect, encouragement, and opportunities they need to build the knowledge, skills, and attitudes to be successful, contributing members of a global society."
Montgomery County Public Schools, Maryland

"In the Arcadia Unified School District, families and community are partners for student success. The policies, personnel and resources of the Arcadia Unified School District are used to ensure that all students are provided engaging, meaningful schoolwork that results in challenging them to think and reason, develop ownership for their own lifelong learning, respect diversity, and be contributing members of society."
Arcadia Unified School District, California

"The Northern Ozaukee School District believes that the most promising strategy for achieving the mission is to develop the district's capacity to function as a professional learning community. The District envisions a school system in which the Board, administration, faculty, and staff will:

- Establish a foundation where all students acquire knowledge and the process of learning;
- Actively involve and support all students in meaningful learning;
- Have high academic, social, and moral expectations for all students; and
- Work collaboratively with students, staff, parents, and community."

Northern Ozaukee School District, Wisconsin

are articulating their own futures through a vision. You also are encouraged to go to the NSBA Key Work website (www.NSBA.org/keywork) for more examples and to post your own district's vision. You can ask for comment or feedback on your vision through this website and perhaps build a dialogue with other board members who are grappling with the issue of creating a vision.

FROM VISION TO PRACTICE

Your vision cannot end with a written statement. Organizations that complete the writing process and believe that they have a vision are mistaken. They have a vision statement. Writing is only the beginning. Moving the vision from paper into practice is the real challenge.

A powerful vision should guide the strategic planning process for the school district. After your board and superintendent have disseminated widely the vision statement, you must breathe life into the vision statement by developing a strategic plan. A beautiful vision without a plan to achieve it is like a great movie title with no script.

In creating a strategic plan, the board-staff leadership team must develop a process to identify goals toward the vision as well as strategies to achieve the goals. Staff subsequently is responsible for creating work plans within the strategies; reviewing the goals, strategies, and work plans with the board; and reporting regularly on progress, needs, and adjustments that are necessary to continue movement toward the vision. The process of strategic planning actually follows the "Key Work" model that is laid out in the remainder of this book: set goals (*standards*); measure progress (*assessment*); evaluate success or lack thereof (*accountability*); redirect resources toward the goal (*alignment*); motivate staff and students (*climate*); build partnerships for success (*collaboration and community engagement*); and regularly reevaluate processes and outcomes (*continuous improvement*). And remember that it all comes back to vision.

Your vision also should be reflected in the policies that the board adopts and the procedures that the superintendent and staff develop to implement the policies. A periodic, systematic review of policies to assure consistency with your adopted vision is an affirmative step that signals to the staff, students, and community that the board is committed to its vision.

One of the benefits of the controversial and oft decried No Child Left Behind legislation is that it made sure that all school systems in America focus first on student achievement for all children. Nothing in the legislation limited school districts to the baseline standards required in the law, and many districts have transcended the law's narrow definitions of adequate yearly progress by providing strong and diverse academic programs and measures of success for every student. In this era of public accountability and enforced scrutiny, your vision and planning should go beyond what the law requires and expand your district's sights to a broad range of measures and opportunities for success. Your vision and planning, following the model suggested in this book, can lead your district to a program for student success that not only will meet the requirements of NCLB but also will go beyond, to whatever level of excellence you can imagine.

WHERE TO BEGIN?

Try the self-assessment in the next section to help determine whether your board already has processes in place to work through each of these stages and is ready to build its vision. Perhaps your visioning process is already complete and you are ready to proceed to the strategic planning for implementing your vision. If so, move to the next chapter on standards or to a Key Action chapter that reflects a more immediate challenge for your district. If you would like to know more about building a shared vision or strategic planning, consult your state school boards association. Your state association can provide these services or offer guidance on various consultants and the quality of their work. Also, consider whether you may have staff within the district who can use or modify the strategies provided by your state association and serve as facilitators for the process. State associations often can provide suggestions and support for those who do not wish to turn the process over to an external resource.

In addition to a self-assessment, the following pages contain other resources to board members working on the visioning process:

- Questions that provide the basis for dialogue among board members and between the board and the superintendent.

- Differentiated responsibilities of the board and the superintendent in the vision-setting process.

- A suggested list of topics that might appear on the board's agenda as a vehicle for addressing a particular Key Work dimension.

- Considerations for the student achievement planning teams to make as they develop an action plan to jump-start the comprehensive student achievement planning process back in their home districts.

Each succeeding chapter contains a similar list of tools and resources for board members and the planning team to use.

VISION SELF-ASSESSMENT

Use this tool to assess your initial understanding of vision and also to get a sense of where you are as a board on this key action.

Indicate the degree to which your board/district has achieved the following elements for establishing a vision for improving student achievement.

4	3	2	1
Fully Achieved	Mostly Achieved	Partially Achieved	Beginning to Achieve

4 3 2 1
Our board has established a written vision that commits to student achievement as the top priority of the school board, staff, and community.

4 3 2 1
Stakeholder representatives (school board, senior leadership, district staff, school staff, employee organizations, parents, community advocates, higher education, business leaders, and students) helped create the vision.

4 3 2 1
As a board we have discussed the core beliefs and values of our school district and community, and these values are reflected in our vision.

4 3 2 1
Our vision is clearly articulated and known to all stakeholders in the community.

4 3 2 1
We frequently revisit and reaffirm our vision to ensure our constancy of purpose.

4 3 2 1
Our vision is the basis for our strategic planning and policy decisions.

4 3 2 1
Our vision is the guiding principle for how we operate as a district.

4 3 2 1
We base our resource and budget decisions on our vision.

4 3 2 1
Everything we do as a board of education aligns to achieve our vision.

VISION QUESTIONS THE SCHOOL BOARD SHOULD ASK ITSELF:

- How do we play a central role in fostering and guiding community dialogue about the vision for its schools?
- How do we define and identify key stakeholders to be involved in the process of creating a vision (e.g., staff, parents, students, community organizations, school site councils, union representatives, higher education, business)?
- How do we know that the district's vision and mission reflect the student achievement expectations and needs of the community?
- In what ways do the school board and superintendent work together to communicate the vision and make it a reality?
- What part does the vision play in the district's strategic plan?
- What policies need to be in place to support our vision?
- How do we continuously assure our vision is future focused?
- How will we know when we are making progress in achieving our vision?

VISION QUESTIONS THE SCHOOL BOARD SHOULD ASK THE SUPERINTENDENT AND STAFF:

- In what ways will we engage the community in the visioning processes?
- How do we assure that we engage participants who represent the entire community?
- How will staff communicate the vision to all stakeholders?
- How do the superintendent and staff use the vision statement as a guide to planning and action?
- What resources are needed to make this vision a reality?
- How will we know when we are making progress in achieving our vision?

PLANNING TEAM CONSIDERATIONS FOR DEVELOPING A PLAN FOR A VISION

1. How will we:
   - Identify and choose someone to facilitate the vision-setting process with the board, staff, and community?
   - Ensure that the vision-setting process includes involvement of all stakeholders in our district?
   - Determine where we are as a district at the start of the process?
   - Set a timetable for completion of key tasks and a target date for completion of the entire vision-setting process?
   - Ensure that our core values are articulated and reflected in the vision and mission?

2. How can we create a process that will reflect the multiple perspectives of our different stakeholders?

ROLES OF THE BOARD AND THE SUPERINTENDENT IN THE VISION AND PLANNING PROCESS

THE SCHOOL BOARD	THE SUPERINTENDENT
1. Approves a strategic planning process to include stakeholders in creating the vision for student achievement.	1-A. Recommends a visionary strategic planning process to the board that incorporates participation by a broad base of stakeholders. 1-B. Ensures the integrity of the planning process. 1-C. Ensures staff development to carry out the planning process. 1-D. Ensures that the recommendations of the strategic planning team are presented to the board for action. 1-E. Coordinates periodic review of the strategic plan.
2. Adopts the vision.	2-A. Ensures that short- and long-range plans related to the vision are developed and carried out both at the district and at the school level. 2-B. Develops performance indicators based on data to measure progress toward vision for student achievement. 2-C. Conducts work sessions with the board to increase its understanding of progress needed to move from current status to vision for student achievement. 2-D. Recommends performance indicators for board action.
3. Adopts board goals that support the vision.	3-A. Works with the board to identify its role in supporting the vision. 3-B. Works with the board to develop plans for carrying out its goals.
4. Communicates the vision.	4-A. Communicates, through the district's communication plan, the vision to the staff and community in a team approach that incorporates board participation. 4-B. Prepares and disseminates information about progress toward the vision.
5. Keeps vision at the forefront of all decision making.	5-A. Uses the vision to guide priority recommendations to the board. 5-B. Uses the vision to guide decisions throughout the organization.
6. Adopts policies needed to achieve the vision.	6-A. Recommends policies needed to support the vision. 6-B. Conducts periodic review with the board to identify additional policies or revise existing ones.
7. Allocates resources based on the vision.	7-A. Recommends resources needed to support the vision through the budgeting process. 7-B. Conducts periodic review with the board to identify resources and funding needed.
8. Monitors progress toward vision periodically.	8-A. Brings data to the board periodically that enables the board to review progress in student achievement. 8-B. Recommends changes based on data.

POSSIBLE AGENDA ITEMS RELATING TO VISION

A. Dialogue and work session with staff and community representatives to create Vision and Mission statements
B. Formal adoption of Vision and Mission statements and establishment of yearly goals
C. Discussion and action on the superintendent's recommended strategic plan for the district
D. Strategic Plan Review
   ✓ Are we meeting our timetable?
   ✓ Plans for assessing successes and shortcomings
   ✓ Yearly update of district's goals
E. Community open forum on the district's vision, mission, and goals
F. Reports from community advisory committees
G. District's communications plan and public relations activities
H. Recognition events for students and staff who exemplify the district's vision
I. Superintendent's report on school improvement plans

3. STANDARDS

Re-reading the chapter on standards in the first edition of the Key Work guidebook illustrates most dramatically how expectations and conditions in public education have changed in the last several years. What a difference a decade makes!

In the first edition, the goal of this chapter was to make the case to school board members and superintendents that their districts must establish standards for student achievement even as many individual states were in the process of doing so. In the argument for standards, we cited examples of standards as part of everyday life. They come in many forms. Athletic standards are among the most familiar—qualifying times in order to compete in a particular race is one example. Licensing examinations for professional certification is another. Most manufacturers have standards for their products and inspectors who are responsible for preventing inferior products and recent events have highlighted how dangerous this world can be when manufacturers among others flout those standards.

Paradoxically, the need for standards in public education had long been debated in education circles and those discussions often devolved into the nature of teaching as art or science and the autonomy of individual teachers. The passage of the No Child Left Behind legislation (NCLB) in 2001 brought a crashing halt to that debate. Game, set, match! NCLB mandated not only use of academic standards but also annual assessment of how well students were doing in meeting those standards. Furthermore, NCLB held schools and districts responsible for their results. And that requirement continues to this day.

As the political climate and leadership in Washington changes can we expect that the original NCLB legislation will change in subsequent reauthorizations? Of course. Will there be modifications to the 2001 legislation? Most certainly, for it is clear that some elements of the original bill simply are not workable and have in some cases stymied state efforts to improve student achievement. NSBA and many others have proposed changes that are being favorably received by lawmakers and others.

With the law changing and evolving in response to our initial experience with its implementation, one thing is clear. Three elements of the original legislation are not going away and should not go away—standards, assessment, and accountability.

These three Key Work areas—standards, assessment, and accountability—will continue to drive many of the decisions required of school boards. In the next three chapters, we will examine each in detail and show how they are fundamental to school improvement and inexorably intertwined. We will begin by examining the status of standards and the role they play in determining the quality of education.

Standards form the foundation for a school district's learning system. They give a common focus to classroom instruction, assessments, and resource use. Standards help teachers and principals set priorities for use of instructional time. Standards provide a measure for identifying students who need extra or different instructional support to succeed. Standards establish consistent expectations so that all children are challenged and receive a quality education.

Currently, states have the responsibility to establish educational standards in the core content areas. As the assessment of state standards evolves and proficiency rates are compared from state to state, we will continue to hear questions about the lack of consistency among these standards. Does a 70 percent proficiency rate for mathematics in Colorado define the same competency and skill set as a 70 percent proficiency rate in Connecticut? Are some states establishing more rigorous requirements for student graduation diplomas than others? Even as we write this second edition, there is talk among governors and others about the need for national standards, a development that NSBA

CHAPTER 3

and most boards of education oppose. Education is a state and local function, and, we argue, needs to remain so. But, unless states and local districts get serious about establishing rigorous standards and collaborating in the process, we can expect that the pressure to develop national standards will increase.

Do we need or want the federal government to establish a single set of national standards for student achievement? Absolutely not. The challenge to states and local boards of education is to heed the lessons learned in the past decade. We will have standards. They are inevitable. The question is who will set them? Unless states and local school boards respond to the "standards setting" challenge, we may well forfeit that authority to external forces.

INCORPORATE STATE STANDARDS INTO OUR INSTRUCTIONAL FRAMEWORK

- Define the standards for student performance

We must be able to explain what we expect each child to know and be able to do at each grade level. That is, we must describe the specific content and skills that the student is expected to demonstrate. This is the "what" of standards. There is a second part to defining student performance. We must also be able to determine the proficiency level we expect a student to meet. In other words, "how well" do we expect the student to be able to perform in order to meet the standards? These expectations should be stated in simple terms with no educational jargon. The standards are not only for educators but also for parents, community, and students. They are the same for everyone.

- Communicate these standards clearly to all stakeholders

Student performance standards must be described in ways that parents, students, community, and staff all would recognize whether students do or do not reach the mark. Too often standards are not concrete and contain statements such as "learn to appreciate literature." How do you measure such a "standard"? What distinguishes those students who have achieved the standard from those who have not? Contrast this with a standard such as "read 20 literary works from a selected list representing a variety of traditional and contemporary literature including novels, folk tales, myths, stories, poems, and plays." Can a group of teachers establish such a list? Can a teacher determine who has met the standard? Can a student understand what is expected? That is not to say that there will not be debate over the list itself or what additional performances are essential beyond just reading a specified number of books. There may even be debate over the appropriate number. But once the stakeholders resolve such issues, the progress of a student toward achieving the standard can be assessed and evaluated.

Some state standards are broadly worded and may even recur from grade to grade. This is often the case with literacy standards. Such an example would be "Blend initial letter-sounds with common vowel spelling patterns to read words." This same state standard occurs in grades one, two, and three. The district must assume the responsibility of "unpacking" that standard. It must describe in complete detail not only how that standard looks in grade one versus grade three, but also what it looks like in the first quarter of the year, the second, the third, and the fourth. Without that clarity teachers are left to their own judgment as to a student's level of success.

Well-developed standards include not only descriptions of the student performance expected but also examples of student work with evaluative comments. Such information provides clear guidance for teachers about how to spend instructional time, how to evaluate students' progress, and what feedback is needed for students to be successful. Parents also learn through concrete examples what the expectations are for their children. And, most importantly, students can see what is required of them.

DISTRICTS SHOULD ESTABLISH THEIR OWN LOCAL STANDARDS

The mandate of state standards does not relieve local school districts of the responsibility for establishing their own district standards. It is certainly not the responsibility or the role of board members to define learning standards. This highly technical, professional responsibility is the work of the superintendent and staff. It is, however, the governance role of the board to ensure that this process takes place.

The rigor and complexity of state standards varies and should be viewed by local school districts as a floor rather than a ceiling. Indeed, school boards and district leadership need to be reminded that the failure of local districts to establish standards on their own contributed to criticism of public education and to the call for national educational legislation. How do we ensure that the standard is the right one? What should board members look for in their governance role of reviewing and approving standards?

- **The standards must be reasonable**

Reaching for the stars is one thing; branding as failures all who cannot touch the stars is quite another. We all want to raise the bar, but setting it at a height that is unattainable will create frustration and defeat. Adults sometimes forget what it was like to be a third-grader. Many have an inflated view of what they actually knew and were able to do at that time of their lives. In fact, few politicians who vote to set educational standards ever attempt to test themselves on the measures. School board members should consider taking the actual student assessments. Such an activity can help build understanding of what we are asking children

to know and be able to do. It also can serve as quite a reality check.

School boards should resist setting very high standards solely for bragging rights. While this approach may be politically popular in some states and districts, it is counterproductive for students and teachers. It sets them up for failure. When students fail to meet the standards, who are the losers and who takes responsibility for their loss?

Adults who advocate for high standards need to understand what it takes for students to reach them. Standard-setting decisions need to be based on sound educational research and knowledge of what is developmentally appropriate performance at each age and stage of development. This is where the professional educators must assume primary responsibility.

- **The standards must challenge the student**

Just as we can err on the side of setting standards too high, we also can end up setting such minimal standards that they become meaningless. To use another athletic analogy, if the high-jump bar is set only a few inches above the ground, all can meet the standard but few will actually have to push themselves to complete the jump. A tendency to set minimal standards is more common with schools and districts that serve a large number of needy students. Educators and local boards may not have sufficiently high expectations for student performance in these communities. They may underestimate student potential, and these lower expectations translate into lower standards. One result is that many students are not challenged and supported to achieve the academic rigor they need to succeed in the competitive world they will enter. School boards must be aggressive in promoting equity and educational excellence for all students. Standards are an essential step.

- **Local standards should incorporate state standards**

Some national organizations have developed standards and curricular guidelines for student performance. All states have established their own standards for student performance to meet NCLB requirements. The degree of detail can vary greatly, and some states are further along with their development than others. State standards—whatever their developmental status—should be reflected in the local district's standards.

It is essential that state and local standards be consistent. Districts may want to expand their local standards beyond state expectations. They may also want to provide more detailed definitions than their state standards. Both approaches can work well. District leaders should avoid setting local standards that are incongruous with those of the state or that are less demanding. This will lead to confusion among staff and make it difficult to establish accountability for quality education.

- **Local standards should prepare students for the changing world**

School districts need to critically examine their standards to ensure that they are reflective of our changing world. The information age and connectivity to a global society have dramatically altered the world in which our students will work and live. The knowledge and skills that served the workers of the industrial era will not be sufficient or appropriate for the knowledge workers of the information age. Knowledge workers will require analytic skills, technology skills, and self-discipline in addition to the traditional foundational academic skills and knowledge. Knowledge workers will be paid for their products, not for their time. Given those significant workforce shifts, school district leaders should examine their graduation standards. The demonstration of acquired skills and knowledge should take precedent over the traditional time units for awarding graduation credits. Competency should replace seat time as the standard criteria for graduation. Standards that are not up-to-date with the competitive workplace will serve neither our students nor our society.

STANDARDS NEED BROAD PUBLIC SUPPORT

School boards cannot establish a successful standards-based educational system without the support of all critical stakeholders. If teachers do not own the standards, they will not prepare their students to meet them. Parents who do not understand and support the standards cannot help their children meet expectations. If the community does not support the standards, it will not provide the resources necessary for schools to prepare students to meet them. Accountability is essential to maintaining public confidence, and it begins with shared understanding of desired results. Mutually agreed upon standards define those expectations. They set consistent levels of performance for all students. Standards are the foundation of quality educational programs.

STANDARDS SELF-ASSESSMENT

Use this tool to assess your initial understanding of standards and also to get a sense of where you are as a board on this key action. Indicate the degree to which your board/district has achieved the following elements for establishing standards for student achievement.

4	3	2	1
Fully Achieved	Mostly Achieved	Partially Achieved	Beginning to Achieve

4 3 2 1
Our district has established student performance standards that clearly define what students are supposed to know and be able to do at each grade level.

4 3 2 1
Our local standards incorporate state standards for student performance.

4 3 2 1
We have local standards that extend the state standards to reflect our community expectations for student achievement.

4 3 2 1
Our standards are published in a single document for distribution to the public.

4 3 2 1
Our standards are written in a format that is easily understood by parents and the community.

4 3 2 1
Our district has a plan for keeping standards in front of parents, students, and staff so that everyone knows what is expected.

4 3 2 1
Our instructional framework is aligned with local and state standards for student performance.

4 3 2 1
We have a process for reviewing and revising our district standards so that they remain current.

STANDARDS QUESTIONS THE SCHOOL BOARD SHOULD ASK ITSELF

- How do we determine that our local standards incorporate state standards?
- How do we communicate standards to students, parents, teachers, and other members of the community?
- How do we determine that the rigor of our standards is consistent with parent and community expectations?
- What do we do as a board to foster and sustain public support for standards?
- How do we determine what policies and resources are needed for the superintendent and staff to implement an instructional program based on our standards?
- What have we done as a board to promote involvement of the community—including business, political, and higher education leaders—in setting standards for our students?

STANDARDS QUESTIONS THE SCHOOL BOARD SHOULD ASK THE SUPERINTENDENT AND STAFF

- Do our standards define both what students should know and what they should be able to do?
- How do we ensure that our standards are congruent with state standards?
- Are state standards used as benchmarks to compare and align district standards but not to limit them?
- How do we determine that teachers understand the standards and have the skills to enable students to achieve them?
- What training and other resources does the staff need to successfully implement standards?
- What percentage of students meets standards, exceeds them, or fails to attain them, and what are their demographics?
- What interventions are in place to assist students who fail to meet the standards?
- How do we help parents know what they can do to help their children attain standards?

PLANNING TEAM CONSIDERATIONS FOR REVIEWING AND REFINING OUR STANDARDS

How can we develop a process that will help us accomplish the following:

- Ensure that our current standards are congruent with state standards.
- Ensure that our local standards extend state standards to specific grade-level expectations.
- Decide where we will begin the process if our district does not have standards in each subject for each grade level.
- Develop a realistic time frame for standards development and implementation.
- Identify the resources that will be needed to develop meaningful standards.
- Build on standards work that already has been done by other districts and by national organizations.

POSSIBLE AGENDA ITEMS RELATING TO STANDARDS

A. Review of the board's policy on standards: Do we have/need one?

B. Presentations by staff:
   - ✓ Our current standards in various subjects
   - ✓ How these standards were determined
   - ✓ How these standards compare to state standards and to those recommended by national organizations

C. Board adoption of subject standards

D. Review of staff development plans for instructional staff

E. Discussion of parent support programs available to enable parents to help students meet academic standards

F. Review of district data on "highly qualified" teachers

ROLES OF THE BOARD AND THE SUPERINTENDENT IN THE STANDARDS PROCESS

THE SCHOOL BOARD	THE SUPERINTENDENT
1. Approves standards for student learning.	1-A. Recommends standards for student learning based on state standards. If no state standards exist, presents standards recommended by a credible external source or presents standards developed locally with input from key stakeholders. 1-B. Leads discussion with the board on state standards and alignment where local standards also exist. 1-C. Leads discussion with the board on whether a commitment exists to exceed state standards. 1-D. Recommends changes to the board as needed.
2. Ensures that curriculum, instruction and assessment are aligned with student achievement standards.	2-A. Implements alignment of curriculum, instruction and assessment with student achievement standards. 2-B. Makes staffing and resource allocation decisions based on student achievement standards. 2-C. Ensures professional development so that teachers incorporate student achievement standards into classroom instruction.
3. Adopts and revises policies to support standards.	3-A. Recommends policies needed to support standards. 3-B. Conducts periodic review with the board to identify additional policies or revise existing ones.
4. Participates in periodic work sessions to review student standards and the district's initiatives to help all students achieve.	4-A. Provides the board with background and updates on district standards. 4-B. Provides the board with data that analyzes the district's efforts to have all students meet standards. 4-C. Discusses and recommends changes to help students who are not meeting standards.
5. Ensures clear, jargon-free communications about standards that increase the awareness and understanding of parents, students and staff.	5-A. Develops a comprehensive communication plan for standards that addresses information needs of parents, staff, students and community. 5-B. Prepares easy-to-understand materials targeted for various audiences. 5-C. Develops talking points about standards to guide board members and staff in presenting and discussing standards to various audiences.
6. Encourages community support for standards.	6-A. Develops materials specifically to help board members serve as advocates for standards within the community. 6-B. Develops materials specifically to help school and district staff serve as advocates for standards within the community. 6-C. Advocates support for standards publicly and privately.
7. Provides resources needed to increase the number of students meeting standards.	7-A. Makes recommendations for budget, allocation of resources, professional development and additional instructional materials and equipment based on data related to the needs of students not meeting standards.
8. Ensures that instructional programs are evaluated for effectiveness in helping students meet standards.	8-A. Evaluates instructional programs periodically for effectiveness in helping students meet standards. 8-B. Sets benchmarks and performance indicators for progress over time. 8-C. Collects data on progress toward benchmarks and performance indicators and reviews periodically with board and with staff. 8-D. Recommends additions or deletions to instructional programs based on periodic evaluations and implements approved changes.

4. ASSESSMENT

No component of Key Works has evolved more in the past decade than assessment. In 1999 we wrote about the need for school boards and school districts to develop a comprehensive assessment infrastructure in order to measure student results. At that point the most prevalent type of assessment occurred in the classroom level in the form of teacher-made tests. Teacher judgment determined the content and grading standards. Some districts established percentages to be used to determine student grades, but the content of the assessments still remained the responsibility of the teachers. Few school districts maintained uniform comprehensive assessment programs.

As the movement toward more standards-based education grew, many states developed testing programs. For the most part, these programs amounted to achievement tests designed to measure student progress on state learning standards. Other states required all districts to administer standardized tests, such as the Iowa Test of Basic Skills. Most of these programs were administered at selected grade levels such as three, five, and eight, or four, eight, and 10. Fewer than 20 percent of the states had annual assessment measures of individual student progress. In a very small number of states these programs were high-stakes with rewards or consequences for schools and school districts.

The passage of No Child Left Behind (NCLB) in 2001 changed the role and the importance of standards and assessment in public education. The law required all states to define standards and to develop annual measures of student achievement in reading and in mathematics for all students in grades three through eight. Many states struggled to put such standards and assessments into place. Some chose to administer existing norm-referenced tests. States had to establish standards and proficiency targets for all schools and report the results on an annual basis. These proficiency targets were determined based on a progression of growth that would ensure that 100 percent of the students would be proficient by the year 2014. Meeting these targets became the basis for determining Adequate Yearly Progress (AYP). Public reporting requirements and the penalties attached for failure to meet AYP gave a new urgency to assessment.

Fear of failure to meet AYP targets caused some districts to make assessment the driving force for instruction. In fact, many complained that spending so much time preparing for tests left no time to teach. The important balance for educators and leaders to understand is that assessment and instruction can no longer be treated separately. Assessment is more than the final step in the instructional program. Measuring how well students are learning must be integrated into the instructional process. Assessment provides feedback for the teacher about student progress and the need for individual interventions. Assessment must inform instruction, not drive it.

Assessment has traditionally been treated as a highly specialized area of education too complicated for all but the "experts." Let us dispel the mystique of assessment for you. Too many testing programs are confusing to the average parent or community member. Complicated terminology and statistics become the focus of discussion rather than the content or purpose of the tests themselves. The critical role of assessment for the learning process requires that all of us have a clear understanding of educational testing programs. What are basic components of a sound assessment infrastructure that school board members should understand and promote?

BASIC COMPONENTS OF A SOUND ASSESSMENT SYSTEM

- Multiple assessments are used to determine student progress

Most states use a single high-stakes test given annually throughout the student's educational experience. These

CHAPTER 4

test results in turn are used to determine everything from student eligibility for graduation to school effectiveness. While such a testing program may be easy to administer, it also can be misleading. There is no one perfect test that produces all the information needed to measure student achievement or school quality. School districts must look beyond the state testing program and incorporate other measures of student learning.

Some tests only measure knowledge. They determine what facts the student has learned (or at least memorized) at that point. These tests can vary widely in degree of difficulty. Just like television quiz shows, the questions can run the gamut from minimal common knowledge to obscure facts known by a few experts. Other tests are designed to measure skills, a timed typing test, for example. Still other tests try to determine the student's capacity to apply skills as well as knowledge to solve problems and specific tasks.

These performance assessments (sometimes referred to as alternative or authentic assessments) also can have varying degrees of difficulty. Some require only basic understanding and skill acquisition for successful task performance. Others demand higher-order thinking skills such as analy-

sis and synthesis in order to solve the problems. The challenge for school districts is to determine the right fit when selecting assessments for measuring student achievement.

- **The assessment program is aligned with the academic standards**

Such alignment may seem simplistic and obvious, but it is not uncommon for school district testing programs to lack alignment with the curriculum. The most glaring inconsistencies occur when the staff develops a set of academic standards, and the district uses standardized tests developed by external test publishing companies that measure other knowledge or skills. Students, teachers, and principals get caught in the resulting crossfire. Do we teach the district program or do we teach the test? Schools should never have to make that choice. There should be clear understanding of what students are expected to learn and confidence that the assessments used will measure those same learning objectives. When a student takes a test, there should be no surprises. Assessment should not be a game of "gotcha." The purpose of a well-designed assessment program is to determine whether or not the district's curriculum is being taught and learned in the classrooms by individual students.

- **Local district assessment programs complement state assessment programs**

NCLB has mandated statewide testing. Most states develop these tests themselves based on established learning standards. Some states use standardized tests from a national test publisher for all districts. A local district needs to review carefully the test requirements at the state level. Districts cannot simply ignore the state mandates and go ahead and "do their own thing" even if they believe their measures are better than those used by the state. This will create inconsistency between what is taught and what is tested. State testing is required, and results are compared

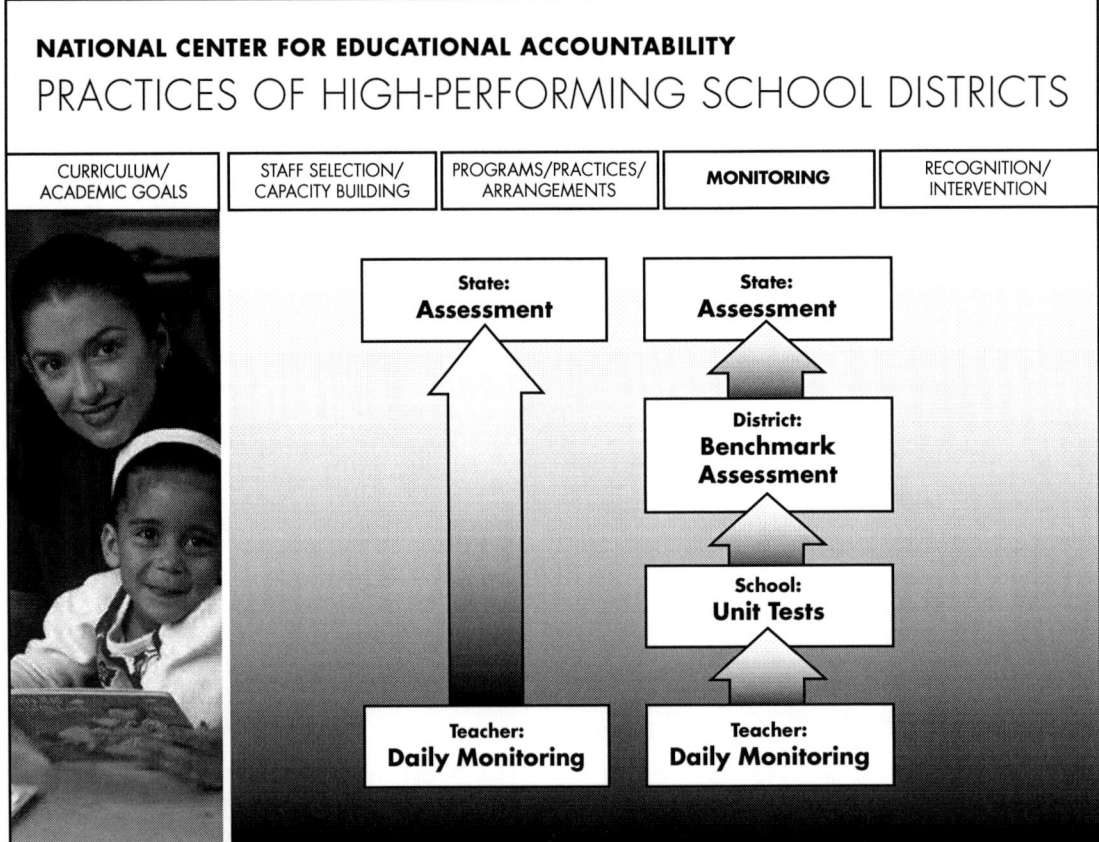

http://www.just4kids.org/en/research_policy/best_practices/framework..cfm

district to district. If your district does not include the state standards and incorporate state testing within your own, your results will suffer in comparison to districts that follow state guidelines. In turn, you may lose public confidence.

At the same time, you should not simply accept state-mandated testing as the only measure of student progress. Your district's standards may exceed those established by the state. In such instances, if you only administer the state's tests, you cannot be sure that the additional learning standards set by your district are actually being taught. The better course of action is to design the district's testing programs to complement those of the state.

- **Local district assessment programs predict readiness for state assessment programs**

School districts must recognize and accept the need to have ongoing assessments administered across the district to determine student readiness for the high-stakes state testing. Studies of high-performing school districts versus low-performing districts show that the way districts treat student assessment is critical to their success on NCLB. Low-performing districts basically leave the day-to-day determination of student mastery to the classroom teacher's independent judgment. Then they administer the state assessment as a separate event and await the results.

High-performing districts, by contrast, incorporate the daily mastery judgment of the classroom teacher, but they do not stop there. In addition to individual classroom measures, teachers share and administer common assessments that they have developed together. The feedback from those measures then guides collaborative instructional decisions and intervention strategies. In turn, common assessments developed by the district are administered across all schools at regular intervals to determine if students are progressing adequately toward the level of proficiency required for success on the state assessments. This type of monitoring is frequently referred to as a "Leading Indicator" system.

- **Local district assessment programs incorporate both "lagging" and "leading" indicators to monitor student results and inform instruction**

What are lagging and leading indicators and how are they used? Lagging indicators are those assessments that are the final measures of student mastery. They are like the final score of the game. The game is over and you determine winners and losers. They are named lagging because they frequently are not provided in immediate feedback form. This is certainly the case with most of the state assessments. The time lapse between when these measures are administered and when the results are announced can be extremely long—weeks, even months. In some states there is great frustration about the fact that actions are required when the accountability standards are not met, and yet, the results are received too late to take timely action. An example would be a state that requires remediation coursework for students who fail to meet the proficiency standard, but the results from the state test do not come back to the schools until after schedules for the coming year are already built and students have been assigned their classes.

Leading indicators, on the other hand, are derived from assessments that are administered at regular intervals throughout the year. They are designed to predict the readiness of students for high-stakes tests administered at a particular time. The feedback from leading indicators is immediate and can be used by teachers and principals to take actions that maximize student learning. Interventions for students struggling to meet mastery levels can be put in place for immediate support. Students who have achieved mastery can be advanced without unnecessary repetition of materials. Leading indicators enable teachers to make informed and deliberate decisions about appropriate learning experiences for individual students.

Both lagging and leading indicators can be used to improve student achievement and are best used when examined together. Using a medical analogy, lagging indicators are like autopsies. We can learn much from detailed examination of the corpse as to what may have caused the death. We might even learn things that help us prevent similar deaths. What we cannot do is change the result.

Leading indicators by contrast are much more like EKGs and blood tests. They constantly monitor the current status of the patient or, in this case, the student. We know from past experience and research that certain indicators are strong predictors of future problems. By providing interventions we can frequently prevent those problems from occurring. We can change results.

The medical adage that an ounce of prevention is worth a pound of cure applies as well to education. Extensive information gathered through a thorough analysis of lagging indicators together with careful monitoring of leading indicators serve as predictors and promote effective intervention.

Lagging indicators are assessments "of" learning. Leading indicators are assessments "for" learning. Both are necessary.

- School board members are familiar with the basic types of tests and their formats

Tests serve different purposes and take on different forms. The terminology can be very confusing to people not trained in educational assessment. It is not necessary to understand all of the specifics in great detail in order to make good policy decisions. There are, however, some basic categories of assessment that school board members should understand. Frequently, testing programs use one format for K-8 and a different format for high school. The major difference is that K-8 assessment is done by grade level, while high school assessment is based on individual course examinations. Let's look at the three common types of assessment: norm-referenced tests, criterion-referenced tests, and performance tests.

NORM-REFERENCED TESTS

Norm-referenced tests compare performance of students against other students. The most familiar format is the standardized norm-referenced test. These tests are developed by a variety of nationwide testing companies. A few of the most widely used are:

- Stanford Achievement Test (SAT)
- Comprehensive Test of Basic Skills (CTBS)
- Metropolitan Achievement Test (MAT)
- California Achievement Test (CAT)
- Iowa Test of Basic Skills (ITBS).

Norm-referenced tests are first given to a large, nationwide sample of students. The scores of these students are then ranked from highest to lowest. The "norm" of the test is the middle score over the entire range of score samples. This norm is called the 50th percentile. By definition, percentile norming guarantee winners and losers—half the students are always above the norm (above average) and half are below. Scoring at the 60th percentile does not mean that the student answered 60 percent of the questions correctly. It means that this student scored as well as or better than 60 percent of the other students who took the same test. A benefit of including some form of norm-referenced testing in a comprehensive assessment program is that it provides an external anchor for comparing student, school, and district performance. The disadvantages to relying exclusively on norm-referenced testing are twofold: 1) the testing may not align well with the learning standards established by the district; and 2) the results are based on comparing student performance, one to another, as opposed to meeting a standard.

CRITERION-REFERENCED TESTS

Criterion-referenced tests (CRT) compare students against a well-defined standard of performance. The effectiveness of this type of assessment is directly related to the clarity of the performance standard. The assessments must match the performance standards. Doing so is not the same thing as simply setting a minimal "cut score" on a given test. Some districts and states have minimal competency levels for certification or graduation requirements. They may contend that they are using a CRT but, in fact, they are simply setting minimal scores on a selected test. School boards need to know the difference.

CRTs frequently are developed at the local level to measure student progress on district standards. The advantage of CRTs is that they can provide a direct match with the district's standards. Another advantage of CRTs over norm-referenced tests is that CRTs can be used to evaluate programs and district initiatives. Not all districts have the capacity to develop comprehensive criterion-referenced assessment programs. Consideration could be given to sharing resources with other districts to collaborate on assessment. Another approach is to begin with an existing test that is most closely aligned with local standards and then to develop supplemental assessments over time to achieve a better overall match.

PERFORMANCE-BASED TESTS

Performance assessments, as the name implies, require students to demonstrate what they can do. Examples of this type of assessment include mathematical computations, problem solving, writing tasks, carrying out science experiments, producing an artistic work, and, in each instance, explaining the work. Collections, referred to as portfolios, of this work are often maintained to demonstrate progress over time.

Performance assessments are more time-consuming and complicated to score than norm-referenced or criterion-referenced tests. They do, however, provide a more complete picture of students' capacities to understand and apply the content and skills that they have learned. Teachers who use performance assessment as an ongoing process and provide feedback to students can significantly improve student performance.

The greatest difficulty in using performance testing is that the rating of performance may not be consistent from one teacher to another. To use performance-based assessment effectively, a district must invest heavily in teacher training not only for delivery of instruction but also for determining student proficiency. There must be agreement on what is expected and a consistent expectation for performance among all teachers.

- **Assessment is necessary but not sufficient for quality assurance**

School boards cannot assume that learning will follow if they give students the right tests. Good assessments accurately measure and report student performance and progress. Actually improving performance, however, requires more than keeping score. Using the assessment results, giving quality feedback, and making changes based on the feedback are essential to improving student achievement. Acting on results is the basis of accountability for quality assurance. Such actions are dependent upon quality results. Quality results require quality assessment. Assessment is not the only step, but it is the first step.

ASSESSMENT SELF-ASSESSMENT

Use this tool to assess your initial understanding of assessment and also to get a sense of where you are as a board on this key action. Indicate the degree to which your board/district has the following elements for establishing an assessment program for improving student achievement.

4	3	2	1
Fully Achieved	Mostly Achieved	Partially Achieved	Beginning to Achieve

4   3   2   1
We have an assessment program that is based on our district's student performance standards.

4   3   2   1
Our assessment program has multiple measures that are administered throughout the year.

4   3   2   1
Our assessment program measures both knowledge and skills.

4   3   2   1
Our assessment program measures more than minimal competency levels.

4   3   2   1
Our assessment program monitors readiness for state assessments.

4 3 2 1
Board members are familiar with the types of tests used in the district, including both content and format.

4 3 2 1
Assessment data are provided to parents and students in a format that is easily understood.

4 3 2 1
Assessment data are provided to teachers and principals in a format that can be used to make informed instructional decisions.

4 3 2 1
Reports of assessment data are provided to the community.

Assessment Questions the School Board Should Ask Itself

- What policies and resources do we have in place to ensure quality assessment in our district?

- How do we know whether or not our student assessments are aligned with state and district standards?

- How do our assessments relate to our vision and student achievement goals?

- How do we know what our assessments measure?

- How do we know how our test results are benchmarked—compared to the state as a whole, to districts with similar demographics, to neighboring districts, and/or to our performance in previous years?

- What do assessments tell us about student performance relative to our short- and long-term goals?

- What assessment reports do we receive, and do we understand how to interpret them and use them to make decisions?

Assessment Questions the School Board Should Ask the Superintendent and Staff

- At what intervals are assessments conducted?

- Are they conducted often enough to give teachers timely information for modifying instruction?

- Does our assessment program use multiple measures of student achievement?

- What subjects are covered in state and district assessments?

- What types of assessments are used—norm referenced, criterion referenced, performance based? What do these terms mean?

- Do tests require the use of a variety of skills, e.g., memorization, analysis, application, communication?

- Does our assessment data provide information on individual students, classrooms, and school performance?

- How do we analyze assessment data to inform instruction, supervision, administration, and policy making?

Planning Team Considerations for Implementing an Effective Assessment Program

1. What is the current state of our testing program?

    - What are the most commonly used assessment measures in our district?

    - Do our tests measure both knowledge and skills?

    - Which tests are norm-referenced? Criterion-referenced?

    - Are our assessments tied to district standards?

    - What is the frequency of test administration?

    - How is staff trained to measure student progress?

    - How do our assessments measure individual student proficiency as well as improvement?

2. How will teachers, parents, and community members be involved in the process?

3. How will we align assessment, curriculum, and professional development to promote student achievement and the district's vision?

4. How will we identify resources needed to develop a quality assessment program?

ROLES OF THE BOARD AND THE SUPERINTENDENT IN ASSESSMENT

THE SCHOOL BOARD	THE SUPERINTENDENT
1. Participates in training to increase understanding of assessment. • Concepts • National and state assessments • Relationship of assessment to standards	1. Holds work sessions with the board explaining all elements of a comprehensive assessment system.
2. Approves and periodically reviews/revises an assessment system for all students.	2-A. Recommends to the board an assessment system that includes multiple assessment measures related to/aligned with standards and vision. 2-B. Uses assessment measures to recommend modifications or changes in curriculum and instruction. 2-C. Incorporates appropriate assessment measures as part of staff evaluations. 2-D. Conducts periodic review of the assessment system with the board and recommends changes.
3. Assures staff development on assessment measures.	3-A. Assures staff development on the district's assessment measures, including use of data and analysis of individual student performance. 3-B. Assures staff development on assessment measures using school and grade-level data.
4. Assures effective, user-friendly communications on assessment measures and progress.	4. Builds understanding, through the district's communications plan, for assessment measures and how they are used to improve instruction.
5. Provides funding to support assessment system.	5. Presents budget recommendations to the board on resources needed to implement and evaluate assessment measures.
6. Approves and monitors policies to assure a strong assessment system.	6-A. Recommends to the board policies to support the district's assessment system. 6-B. Recommends additions or changes as needed.

POSSIBLE AGENDA ITEMS RELATING TO ASSESSMENT

A. Discussion of the board's policy on assessment:
   - ✓ Do we have/need one?
   - ✓ How is its implementation monitored and measured?
   - ✓ Is it consistent with current research findings and best practices?

B. Review of district's assessment program
   - ✓ Roles of both diagnostic assessments and summative testing
   - ✓ Relationship to state testing programs
   - ✓ Review of the yearly testing calendar
   - ✓ Adequacy of resources to develop and maintain quality assessment tools

C. Discussion of role that "voluntary" external testing programs (SAT, ACT, AP, IB, etc.) play in helping the district achieve its goals

D. Report on training and support given to teachers to assure that they use diagnostic assessments as a regular part of instructional planning and implementation

PROFILE OF LEADERSHIP:
5. METROPOLITAN SCHOOL DISTRICT OF WARREN TOWNSHIP

Indiana's Metropolitan School District of Warren Township is an urban education success story. Despite having nearly 60 percent of its students living in poverty, Warren Township, a 12,000-student district comprising the east side of Indianapolis, saw all of its elementary schools make federal Adequate Yearly Progress (AYP) standards in 2007. At some Warren Township schools, the student passing rate on Indiana state exams has climbed from 20 percent in the early part of this decade to 70 percent today.

But for the Metropolitan School District of Warren Township's Board of Education and its superintendent, Peggy Hinckley, reaching this point was hardly an easy process.

In fact, the Warren Township success story owes more to determination than it does to innovation. People in the community and employees of the district initially were resistant to the reforms the board and Hinckley intended to enact. It was only after these methods proved successful that public opinion started to turn.

"The only person who likes change is a wet baby," Hinckley says, describing the reform process and the turmoil it initially created.

In the 1980s, Warren Township and its schools generally were considered desirable places to be. East Indianapolis was a middle-class neighborhood with stable families, and the schools reflected that environment.

But, as in many communities, the middle-class, predominantly white residents gradually moved from the city to the suburbs and the eastern side of Indianapolis became increasingly poor. Today, 58 percent of Warren Township's students qualify for free or reduced-price meals. The district's racial demographics also have shifted. The once-predominantly white district now is 44 percent black and 43 percent white.

Academic performance in the school district gradually had declined as well. By 2001, the Warren Township school district was struggling. That year, the school board brought in Hinckley with a mandate to make changes. Those changes included looking at all the district's practices—academic, organizational and financial—and making tough decisions about what to keep and what to discard.

In particular, Hinckley wanted a more data-driven approach to classroom instruction. That desire immediately put her at odds with teachers, who balked at what they perceived as micromanagement from the central office.

"Initially, the teachers resented the lack of flexibility," Hinckley says. "It was very hard in the first year."

DATA DRIVES DECISION-MAKING

The new emphasis on data might have upset the teachers, but, as Hinckley says, "one of the reasons the board recruited me was because student achievement was declining."

Student performance on the Indiana Statewide Testing for Educational Progress-Plus (ISTEP), the state's standardizing testing program, declined for three consecutive years between 1999 and 2001. The 2000-01 school year saw the district bottom out, as fewer than half the students passed the standardized tests. At the sixth-grade level, the passing rate was below 40 percent. The passing rates at some individual schools was as low as 20 percent. Warren Township had the lowest overall scores among the Indianapolis area townships.

In addition, the district also faced a financial crunch when Hinckley arrived. The district's cash balance had fallen to dangerously low levels, so one of the new superintendent's first duties was to find $3 million in budget cuts.

CHAPTER 5

School board member Sue Switzer says the board recognized that the district needed a new direction. Board members were unified in that regard, she says.

"When we hired Dr. Hinckley, the board's number one question was, 'What would you do to improve student achievement?'" Switzer says.

Hinckley was a well-known, veteran administrator. Before coming to Warren, she served as superintendent in LaPorte, Ind., for 12 years and, in 1995, was named Indiana's Superintendent of the Year. In 1994, the state superintendent of public instruction appointed her to the Committee to Study Systemic Change for Indiana's Policies for Education. Hinckley brought with her a cache of respect from educators within the state.

She also brought a plan, borrowed from the Brazosport, Texas, schools that she thought would turn Warren Township's struggling fortunes around.

In the 1990s, Brazosport gained national acclaim for its data-driven approach to improving student performance. Today, 400 school districts across the nation use the Brazosport model for school improvement. (However, Brazosport is not longer one of them. Changes in that district's leadership led the school system to abandon the reform plan that once made the district famous.)

This eight-step program calls for:

- Data disaggregation;
- An instructional timeline, or pacing guide for teaching;
- Instructional focus, meaning lessons should target the specific needs of students;
- Assessment of student progress, using regular tests;
- Tutorials for students who don't master skills the first time around;
- Enrichment for those who do;
- Maintenance, or "reteaching", to reinforce skills that have been learned; and
- Continuous monitoring of student progress.

"It's a continuous improvement model based on a continuous stream of data," Hinckley says. Nationally acclaimed educational consultant Patricia Davenport, the former director of curriculum and instruction in Brazosport, has helped the district implement and execute this program, which focuses on reading and math.

In Warren Township, elementary and middle teachers are expected to closely follow a carefully designed plan. For example, 30 minutes every day are spent on remediation or enrichment, or a "success period."

Every three weeks, students are given four-item assessments to gauge their progress. The assessments are color-coded, with red meaning students missed two or more items, yellow meaning they missed one item and green meaning they got all four correct. Teachers and principals also get a class-level picture of student performance.

Students who don't perform well on these mini-assessments are required to attend remedial sessions while their classmates are in physical education or health.

"Assessment drives reform," Hinckley says. "If your assessment data says your students didn't master the standard, rather than wait another semester, you immediately provide help."

CHANGING A CULTURE

Hinckley felt her approach would work. But she also knew that all the planning in the world would be for naught if Warren Township's teachers didn't buy into the program.

Change rarely is easy in public schools. Even the most apparently simple and benign changes often end up scrutinized and criticized. But the resistance Hinckley received from Warren Township's teachers was far more than she or school board members had bargained for.

Many teachers in the district protested what they considered an overly rigid plan. Teachers complained that Hinckley's proposal would take away their decision-making abilities in the classroom.

"They felt we were telling them what to teach, when to teach, and how to teach," Switzer says.

The school board did its best to repair relations with the teachers. They held numerous meetings at the schools to listen to teachers' concerns and solicit input as to how to implement the plan. The board and superintendent also gradually introduced plan by implementing it as a pilot program at three schools. When scores at those three schools increased considerably after that first year, it made the plan an easier sell at the remaining schools, Hinckley says.

But, she says, the most important thing the board did during this turbulent first year was to back the superintendent and the program. Board members told teachers that they were willing to listen to input about the best way to implement the plan, but were firm that the plan itself was going to be implemented, no matter how much consternation it caused among employees.

"They heard the complaints and stood firm," Hinckley says.

As far as the budget cuts, Hinckley considered this an opportunity, not a problem. She, her staff, and the school board carefully reviewed every item in the school district's budget. Items that either weren't working or weren't instructional were cut, and savings were redirected to the classroom.

"There is some money involved (in school reform), but it hasn't been substantial. Mostly, it was reordering priorities," she says.

A LESSON IN CONSISTENCY

The schools in Warren Township began making gradual, steady improvement once the eight-step program was implemented. Schools that once had 20 percent passing rates on state tests now have 70 percent of students passing. And every one of Warren Township's elementary schools met AYP standards during the 2007-08 school year, as did the school district as a whole.

Time—and the district's successes—also have salved the wounds of the teachers who felt undermined in 2001. Hinckley said she no longer hears complaints about the plan from veteran teachers and new hires come in knowing what to expect.

"Now, if we take it away, we'll probably have a mutiny," Switzer says. In fact, some Warren Township teachers now are helping to draft curriculum materials used across the district. Switzer says this is another sign teachers are buying into the program.

However, Switzer says, the program itself, while effective when properly implemented, isn't a guarantee to turn a district around. She says it is far more important for school boards to find a successful approach and stick with it, noting that Warren Township has used the same reform program for seven consecutive years. Consistency, she says, is the key.

"We joke about how we're not doing anything new, but I really do think that's one of the things that has made us successful," says Switzer.

She says the board's strong relationship with the superintendent also has been a strong component in the district's success. The board is unified behind the improvement plan and Hinckley. Switzer said Hinckley's previous experience and proven track record gave board members a level of confidence from the beginning of her tenure.

Next up for Warren Township is transferring the success the district has seen at the elementary school level to the middle and high school ranks. Hinckley says the model hasn't been accepted part of the middle school routine up to this point, but she intends for that to change. Starting this year, if middle school students do not pass the state tests, they must take a remedial schedule with intensive academics and no electives or vocational courses. District officials also added more academics to the school day. In 2004, they made the difficult, and somewhat controversial, decision to eliminate middle school art departments so that the district's limited resources could be applied to academic areas.

"We have started to dismantle the middle school model," Hinckley says. In taking a more academically oriented, data-driven focus to middle school, Hinckley once again is butting heads with teachers and middle school administrators who favor the traditional middle school approach of exploratory learning in a wide range of fields.

Hinckley says, "It doesn't make sense to give a kid cultural literacy if he can't read at grade level."

Hinckley, Switzer, and the other members of Metropolitan School District of Warren Township Board of Education know that continued reform efforts won't be easy. But they have made considerable progress and are determined to build upon what they have done in the past seven years.

"In an urban environment, you can do this. I'm not going to tell you it's easy, but I will tell you there's hope," Hinckley says. "It's a tough business, but it's the noblest work of all."

6. ACCOUNTABILITY

Accountability is one of the most frequently heard words when discussing public education today. Community advocates clamor for it. Politicians promise it. Business leaders criticize the lack of it. Parents demand it from teachers. Teachers demand it from parents. And everyone expects it from students. But what is it?

Accountability means taking your fair share of responsibility for outcomes. Being accountable means that you answer not only for your actions but also for the results of your actions. Accountability includes taking credit for achieving the desired results and accepting responsibility when targets are missed.

In public education all stakeholders share accountability for student success. This balance of responsibility is often difficult to find, especially when results are not what stakeholders had expected. Effective leadership by the school board and the superintendent can establish a shared accountability process that improves student achievement. Shared accountability requires careful delineation of expectations, roles and responsibilities, and agreed-upon measures of success.

This chapter explores the characteristics of a strong accountability structure, a necessary component of a successful school district.

A STRONG ACCOUNTABILITY PROCESS FOCUSES ON STUDENT RESULTS

This accountability era has a specific bottom line—student results. If there was any confusion on this point before, the passage of the No Child Left Behind (NCLB) legislation in 2001 clearly established student results as the basis for public school accountability. This was a new way of thinking for many of us. Public entities frequently measure their effectiveness in terms of inputs. That is, they measure how many individuals are assigned to a task or how many hours are required to complete it. The inference of such reporting is that when more resources are invested in a task or initiative the participants do a better job.

Sometimes results are described in outputs. A checklist of tasks accomplished or work projects completed is offered as evidence of being accountable. Again the quantity of completed activities is used as a measure of how good a job we are doing. For example, schools might report that they doubled the number of after-school tutorials during the past year. Whether or not the tutorials paid off is not part of the equation.

True accountability reports not just input and output. Accountability incorporates the actual outcomes that result from the inputs and outputs. Public entities now are answering to the public in terms of outcomes and results. For public education, that translates to improved student achievement. Accountability is not just about what you did but about what difference it made for your students.

A COMPREHENSIVE DATA COLLECTION PROCESS IS ESTABLISHED TO ANSWER THE QUESTION, "HOW WELL ARE WE DOING?"

Determining results requires having the capacity to ask and answer all kinds of questions about student achievement. The system must be able to account for each and every student. Data are collected and analyzed on individual student progress, school progress, and district progress. Data are disaggregated by gender, race, or other factors that could highlight disparate group results. Access to the data is readily available to all stakeholders. Results are reported in a cumulative format to track progress over time. The final chapter of this book, "Putting It All Together—Being an Information Age Board of Education," goes into the details of what board members can do to ensure that their districts have the capacity to collect and analyze the information they need to be fully accountable to themselves and to their public.

CHAPTER 6

SUCCESS IS MEASURED BY IMPROVED STUDENT ACHIEVEMENT

How we measure student success has changed significantly. Clear standards, together with explicit measures to decide mastery, are the yardsticks for determining student achievement results.

Traditionally, individual student success was measured by comparing a student's performance to the performance others. What quartile did the student fall into? What stanine? What percentile? Was he in the top half? The top 10 percent? Ranking student work (both formally and informally) had been common practice in the past. We all can remember hearing teachers use phrases like "graded on the curve." Such a perspective guarantees winners and losers. Some students will always come out at the top, some in the middle, and some at the bottom. While these are ways of comparing relative performance they are not measures of accountability. A student could be in the bottom of a group's performance and still be very competent. Conversely, a student could have the best performance of the group and yet not be competent. The question is not how the student performs compared to others. The question is how the student performs compared to the performance standard.

Individual student results must be measured against expectations set by clearly defined standards. Educators must be able to answer the question, "Has this student mastered the knowledge and skills expected for academic success?" School boards also must be able to answer, "What percent of our students have achieved mastery?" In order to answer these questions, districts must have in place explicit standards as discussed in Chapter 3 and a solid assessment structure for measuring achievement of these standards as discussed in Chapter 4.

ALL SCHOOL AND DISTRICT DATA ARE PUBLICLY REPORTED IN A STRAIGHTFORWARD, EASY-TO-UNDERSTAND FORMAT

Results are provided to parents in a timely manner. The reporting format should include cumulative data that clearly track the student's progress from year to year. Parents should be able to see how their child's performance compares to district standards. They also should be given information that tells them how their child's performance compares to other students in the same school as well as to students at district, state, and national levels. Most important, parents should be made aware of interventions and supports being implemented if their child's performance does not meet the standards and the extent to which those interventions are moving the child to proficiency.

STUDENT DATA ARE ANALYZED WITH RESPECT TO GROWTH AND IMPROVEMENT, NOT JUST END RESULTS

Multiple data must be collected and analyzed from many perspectives. Certainly proficiency must be measured—how students perform relative to district and state standards. It is also necessary to be able to measure how much academic gain every student makes each year. Measuring this growth is as important as measuring proficiency in setting up an accountability structure. Growth toward proficiency is a more significant measure of school and classroom effectiveness than proficiency alone. Both are needed.

The accountability process must incorporate the capacity to identify whether progress varies among subgroups of students within the total population. Disaggregation of data by race, gender, and socioeconomic factors is essential to identify differential success rates and pinpoint where help is needed. Data must be disaggregated based on demographic subgroups as well as on instructional interventions taken and their impact.

ACCOUNTABILITY IS THE IMPETUS FOR CONTINUOUS IMPROVEMENT

Accountability should not be viewed negatively, though it often is. Accountability is blamed for raising anxiety among teachers. Some parents are concerned that high-stakes tests create undue anxiety in children. They believe that schools create an atmosphere of pressure that is too heavy for children, especially among the younger students. Some schools spend the weeks before high-stakes tests in total drill and preparation. In addition to increasing anxiety among students, these practices bore students with the rote repetition of critical assessment items. Such practices do not represent the intent of a sound accountability structure within the school district.

Research from the National Center for Educational Achievement found that low-performing school districts depend on teachers to determine student mastery on a daily basis. No other measures beyond the teacher's judgment are taken prior to the high-stakes tests. Consequently, individual educators are left to their own devices to prepare students for the annual assessments given by the states. School and district leadership have no clear idea of where students are in their readiness for the tests and, more important, they have no systemic intervention strategies beyond the efforts of the individual teacher.

The same research found that high-performing districts also depend on the daily monitoring of mastery by the classroom teacher; however, they do not stop there. Beyond the classroom teacher's individual judgment, teachers at the same grade level develop common assessments that are given to all students in that school. The results are shared among the teachers and collaborative strategies are implemented when students need additional support. At the district level, in turn, assessments are developed to measure student mastery on the learning standards. Schools monitor how well their common assessments predict results on the district mastery measures. The district monitors how well its measures predict results on the state tests. This type of robust accountability structure informs instruction for all classrooms in the district.

If school districts and staff believe that accountability promotes quality education, they will not create a negative environment for assessment. In fact, they will have such a comprehensive internal accountability process that the high-stakes assessments generated by the state merely will serve as an external confirmation of what the schools and districts already know about how their students are doing.

STUDENT RESULTS ARE INCLUDED AS PART OF STAFF EVALUATIONS

This component is not easy to execute but it is essential to an effective accountability process. If individual teachers, principals, and other staff members are going to be held accountable for student results, it is critical that the staff impact can be fairly measured. An accountability process must take into consideration not only the end results but also where each student began. Two students can end the year at the same achievement level, but they may have begun the year at different levels. Likewise, two students could begin the school year at the same level of achievement but end the year with very different results. In both cases, one student learned more than the other student in one year. This is why annual assessments are so important. If a district doesn't measure student progress annually, it can't determine growth. If the district can't determine annual growth, it can't assess teacher impact. And if the school board can't determine teacher impact, it can't hold teachers or anyone else accountable.

Many factors contribute to students' success or failure. Some students come to school with a background of advantages; others, with disadvantages and burdens that impede their opportunities for success. Despite these differences, success or failure is not predetermined. In fact, patterns of student success or failure frequently can be attributed to individual teachers. Data analysis of student results should be an integral part of the teacher evaluation process. Teachers who consistently produce greater than average student improvement gains should be recognized and should share their expertise with colleagues. Teachers whose students consistently achieve below expectations need to have their teaching strategies carefully analyzed and corrected.

ACCOUNTABILITY DOES NOT LIMIT THE BREADTH AND DEPTH OF THE EDUCATIONAL EXPERIENCE

One criticism of standardized testing is that it limits overall learning opportunities for students. Schools are criticized for having a narrowly focused program of studies that translates into "teaching to the test." Critics believe that only the tested content is being taught to most students. They worry that struggling students are being denied access to the arts, physical education, and other elective subjects. These critics believe that the state assessment programs are counterproductive to providing quality education for children.

School boards must take a strong leadership role in ensuring that a robust and rigorous instructional program is maintained. Certainly, responsible leaders have high expectations for achievement for all students and these expectations are clarified through well-defined curricula and programs. What about schools or districts that do not have those high standards? How do they ensure that all students are provided the opportunity to learn?

National and state accountability measures are a means of protecting students and parents from low expectations in public education. This does not mean that those measures are the only responsibility leadership has for student learning. In a high-quality district, students will excel beyond the minimum standards set by the state. In a high-quality district, learning experiences are never limited to the "tested" measures. In a high-quality district, extensive educational options are available to students not only within the core subject areas but also in the areas of the visual and performing arts, health and physical education, and technology and career opportunities. Accountability measures determined at the state level should serve as a floor, not a ceiling, for the district education standards.

STUDENT RESULTS DRIVE DECISION-MAKING

All public school districts report their student results. If reporting results is the end game, the district does not have an accountability process. Accountability occurs when a district uses the information from student results to make educational decisions. Just as teachers should use data to inform instruction, district leadership should use data to inform their decision-making. Results should be analyzed to determine trends and patterns. In particular, results can identify successful programs as well as programs that need to be improved or eliminated. Accountable district leadership must make difficult decisions to change or to eliminate ineffective programs. With an effective accountability process, these decisions are not based on perceptions and politics, but on facts and focus.

Leaders keep their priorities in focus by constantly asking themselves: "How is this decision going to improve student performance?" They then analyze the data to monitor the effectiveness of their decisions. Success is recognized and rewarded. Lack of success drives visible change and improvement efforts.

Accountability uses data as a tool, not a weapon. When leaders use data to threaten or punish, stakeholders resist examining data for fear of negative findings and consequences. Real accountability is about using data to inform and improve. When data is used as feedback to decide best actions and next steps then, and only then, will true improvement occur.

Finally, examine the accountability measures and actions that board members apply to staff. Would you be willing to be held to these same standards? Do you hold yourselves accountable to the same degree? Are you as board members accountable for student results? If not you, who?

ACCOUNTABILITY SELF-ASSESSMENT

Use this tool to assess your initial understanding of accountability and to get a sense of where you are as a board on this key action. Indicate the degree to which your board/district has achieved the following elements for establishing accountability for improving student achievement.

4	3	2	1
Fully Achieved	Mostly Achieved	Partially Achieved	Beginning to Achieve

4 3 2 1
Our district publishes an annual report of progress.

4 3 2 1
Our annual report includes data on student achievement and district performance related to district goals and standards.

4 3 2 1
The format of our report is consistent from year to year and includes data from prior years.

4 3 2 1
We compare our data with data from other districts that are similar to ours.

4 3 2 1
We examine our data by gender, race, and socioeconomic status to measure the success of all students.

4 3 2 1
We use our student achievement data to make decisions and establish district priorities.

4 3 2 1
We communicate to the public how our decisions are linked to student achievement data.

4 3 2 1
Principals and teachers use student achievement data to make decisions and set instructional priorities.

4 3 2 1
We use our student achievement data to plan staff development and to recognize and reward teacher performance.

4 3 2 1
We tie evaluations of staff and of ourselves as board members to student achievement results.

ACCOUNTABILITY QUESTIONS THE SCHOOL BOARD SHOULD ASK ITSELF

- How do we ensure that our policy and budget decisions are research-based and data-driven?
- How do we recognize and reward students, teachers, and schools that meet or exceed student performance standards?
- What are the consequences and interventions for students, teachers and schools that have not met standards?
- How are achievement measures and results reported to teachers, parents, and the public?
- What role do student achievement results play in the evaluation of the superintendent?
- How does the school board evaluate itself in terms of student achievement?

ACCOUNTABILITY QUESTIONS THE SCHOOL BOARD SHOULD ASK THE SUPERINTENDENT AND STAFF

- Do we have an information system that provides adequate data for accountability?
- How do staff and students understand what is expected of them?
- How is success or failure assessed?
- What are the system's rewards and consequences for success and failure?
- How do student achievement results factor into staff evaluations?
- How are parents encouraged to be responsible partners in their child's education?

PLANNING TEAM CONSIDERATIONS FOR DEVELOPING A PLAN FOR ACCOUNTABILITY

1. What process will we use to determine if the following components are present in our system of accountability?

- Clear accountability for each and every student
- Clear indication of student proficiency
- Method for determining annual student academic growth or improvement
- Capacity to disaggregate student results by race, gender, socioeconomics, or other identifiable groups
- Capacity to measure school effectiveness
- Capacity to tie student progress to individual teachers
- Capacity to incorporate student results as part of staff evaluation

2. What's our timeline for our first steps, and how can we determine what's a reasonable timeframe for having a system of accountability in place?

3. How will we involve teachers, parents, and community members in the accountability process?

POSSIBLE AGENDA ITEMS RELATING TO ACCOUNTABILITY

A. Review the board's policy on accountability:
   ✓ Do we have/need one?
   ✓ How is its implementation monitored?
B. Report and discussion of how we use internal accountability data to prepare our district to meet external accountability requirements
C. Report and discussion of resources provided for staff to analyze and share data on individual students
D. Report and discussion of how we report individual schools' progress data to the public
E. Report and discussion of how supervisors use data in staff evaluations
D. Discussion of the data the board needs to evaluate the effectiveness of programs
E. Public reporting and discussion of Adequate Yearly Progress data

ROLES OF THE BOARD AND THE SUPERINTENDENT IN ACCOUNTABILITY

THE SCHOOL BOARD	THE SUPERINTENDENT
1. Establishes an accountability process with measurable criteria and assures an annual review.	1-A. Recommends an accountability process to the board based on the district's strategic plan, standards and other important factors. 1-B. Leads an annual review of the accountability process and recommends changes based on student performance. 1-C. Assures that data and accountability measures are used at district/school level to set instructional priorities. 1-D. Ensures staff evaluations are linked to accountability measures. 1-E. Requires professional development on the accountability process.
2. Participates in work sessions to understand accountability measures, including data analysis, and how the board, administration and staff should use this information.	2-A. Plans periodic training for the board on accountability measures, including data, its use and application. 2-B. Ensures staff training in use of data and other accountability measures.
3. Ensures that the superintendent's evaluation includes accountability measures.	3. Works with the board to identify accountability measures to be used in the superintendent's evaluation.
4. Recognizes and rewards teachers who consistently produce greater than average student improvement gains.	4-A. Identifies a program to recognize teachers who consistently produce greater than average gains. 4-B. Carries out recognition program.
5. Supports the superintendent's recommendation for when dismissal is warranted.	5-A. Develops a process to identify teachers whose students consistently fail to make expected gains. 5-B. Makes the board aware of district assistance available to these teachers. 5-C. Monitors teachers' progress toward improvement. 5-D. Recommends dismissal or non-renewal.
6. Ensures effective and timely communications on the accountability system and progress.	6-A. Analyzes data and other accountability measures and presents explanation in "user friendly" way to board and to the community. 6-B. Communicates, through the district's communications plan, use of and progress with accountability measures to improve student achievement. 6-C. Assures that an annual report is developed containing data on student achievement and district performance data related to goals and standards.
7. Ensures funding to implement accountability measures.	7. Presents budget recommendations and rationale to the board.
8. Evaluates itself on board goals related to student achievement.	8. Works with the board to develop its evaluation process.
9. Uses student achievement results to drive decision-making	9. Reports all information relative to improved student achievement and makes recommendations on needed changes.
10. Assures compliance with state accountability measures.	10-A. Makes the board aware of any state-mandated reporting requirements for student learning. 10-B. Assures adherence at district/school levels. 10-C. Shares data with the board concerning state mandates.
11. Ensures that parents receive annual personalized data on their children's achievement.	11-A. Develops a system for providing parents with cumulative data that clearly traces individual progress from year to year and shows progress on meeting district standards. 11-B. Assures a system to provide parents whose students fail to meet district standards with information on district resources and alternatives available.

7. ALIGNMENT

Most of us have purchased new tires for a car. The final bill for the work almost always includes charges for wheel balancing and alignment. Most of us do not blink or even question the additional charges because we would not dream of purchasing new tires without having both the balance and alignment checked and recalibrated as needed.

It is interesting that the concept of alignment in other situations receives so little attention. That is certainly true in too many school districts. Part of the problem may be timing. When we drive and the car's wheels are not aligned, the results are troublesome and can be expensive if we ignore them (results). For one thing, if the car is out of alignment, we have to carefully hold the wheel to keep the car from wandering to the right or to the left. If we do not fix the problem, we buy new tires much sooner than expected because of damaging wear patterns.

In organizations such as school systems, lack of alignment can be just as problematic and expensive in its own way, but the effects are often not immediately obvious. When resources, thinking, planning, and execution are aligned, everything goes much more smoothly. Knowing where others stand, what they are thinking, and what we are trying to accomplish makes the work easier and more fulfilling. Alignment fosters a real sense of accomplishment.

Think of a time when you were part of a successful team. Chances are you would describe the experience with these words: open and continuous communication, clarity of and agreement on goals, understanding of roles and responsibilities, as well as a process for completing the work. You remember how smoothly and successfully the work got done. If asked to describe a frustrating team experience, chances are the elements cited above would be absent.

Barriers to alignment are communication and the way work is organized. Typically, in school districts (and most other organizations) major functions are compartmentalized and broken into discrete tasks that are then assigned to individuals to carry out. The implicit assumption is that if everyone does what he or she is assigned to do, the result will be as expected. Absent good channels of communication to go along with work assignments, individuals end up working in isolation, pursuing laudable goals even as their efforts are increasingly divorced from what others are doing and trying to accomplish.

When this happens the typical result is what some individuals refer to as "random acts of improvement." For example, if I am the science supervisor, I will try to get as much attention as possible focused on science programs and on the resources needed to implement them. And why shouldn't I? That's my job.

Or is it? The problem is that's what every other supervisor is also trying to accomplish for his/her field of specialization. This pursuit by individuals all acting in good faith creates a kind of "silo" mentality in which none of them is focused on the instructional program as a whole and how it is best configured and coordinated to achieve the district's student performance goals.

Peter Senge, in his classic book, *The Fifth Discipline*, describes a simulation used at the Massachusetts Institute of Technology called the Beer Game. The simulation involves three players: a manufacturer, a distributor, and a retailer. The tendencies of those who play the game are twofold: first, they focus on playing their positions (that is, pursuing their best interests) without considering how what they are doing is affecting the other players. Secondly, they communicate only sporadically and in limited ways. Almost every time the game ends in great frustration among the players. Typically, each player ends up with more of a particular beer than he or she wants or can sell. The lessons of the Beer Game are: 1) No one wins unless everyone wins, and 2) communication is essential to

CHAPTER 7

creating a win-win situation. These two lessons are essential to understanding alignment and its importance to the work of school boards and school districts.

If alignment enhances productivity and progress, what will help boards and school systems practice it? A good place to begin is by establishing clarity and consensus about system goals and priorities. Alignment is enhanced when the board, working with the superintendent, staff, and community, establishes clear goals and priorities reflecting community expectations as well as state and federal requirements. It is a little like the car we talked about earlier that works more efficiently and effectively when it is aligned.

Another way to think about alignment is to examine the district's established channels of communication. Are discussion, reflection, and collaboration among staff encouraged? In other words, do people talk to each other regularly about what they are doing and how they are contributing to improved student and school system performance? Without ongoing communication about priorities, goals, actions and results, alignment may remain always just out of reach.

Let's take an example and explore it in some detail. Suppose that one of the goals of the system is to improve the transition of students from middle school to high school. Suppose further that we have data that confirms that many students do not make that transition well; they become lost, fall behind, fail their course work, and drop out.

Turning that situation around is a challenge that has implications for the whole school system. What, for example, can the board do to increase the chances of success for students moving from middle to high school? That same question can be asked of every principal, supervisor, and staff member in the school system. Each can and should play a role in the successful achievement of this goal. The question properly asked and explored in a spirit of collaboration, not finger-pointing, can move the system toward greater alignment.

Asking the right questions at the right time can become the basis for bringing people together to develop a plan that delineates tasks to be accomplished as well as specific roles and responsibilities. If that process engenders widespread involvement, alignment will be one of the most important outcomes.

In this case, what role can the board play in moving the system toward greater alignment? One of the most important strategies available is to ask the right questions. These questions will frame the challenges and set expectations regarding the kind of information that the board will want from staff as the initiative proceeds. For example, the board many ask: What kind of changes will be needed in key program areas such as the science program? The English program? The mathematics program? At still another level, what are the implications for student scheduling? Facilities? Transportation? Resource allocation? Teacher selection and training? And so forth. Asking pointed question that will require thinking and planning on the part of staff is not micromanaging. It is a legitimate and important role for the board to play. Such questions should encourage staff come together to address the common challenge and come up with ways to coordinate their work. When that happens, real progress becomes possible.

Another key consideration for the board as it pursues alignment is resource allocation. The traditional thinking about school budgets holds that 93 percent of the typical district budget is driven by fixed costs such as transportation, salary, and benefits. That leaves about 7 percent available to the board to achieve its vision and goals for improving student achievement. As with most bits of conventional wisdom, there is some truth to this observation. It is also true that how you use those discretionary resources will determine how closely you can come to achieving your stated goals.

The caution here is not to automatically assume that 7 percent figure to be sacrosanct. In fact, the board and the school system have a good deal of discretion in how that 93 percent of the budget is to be used. Staffing is just one example. Many systems, for example, allocate staff based on fixed formulae (27:1 student-teacher ratio) often in the name of equity even when doing so may not reflect or support board priorities. If reading on grade level by grade three is a system priority, elementary school staffing should reflect that priority, which may translate into adjustments in staffing in other areas. Still other systems have no formula and allocate based on a combination of past practice and the "squeaky wheel" syndrome. One system of allocating staff is not better than another, but the board should ask and understand the basis upon which staffing allocations are being made and how they are aligned with the board's priorities.

Even if, as a board, you have not yet clearly identified goals and priorities, the budget proposed by the superintendent almost certainly is based on some rationale. In the best of all worlds, it is better to go through the goal-setting exercise before taking up the proposed budget. But, in the real world, events and schedules sometimes force provisional measures. Asking the superintendent to align his or her budgetary recommendations based on his and the staff's needs analysis and priorities can begin a fruitful conversation and emphasize the board's determination to make deliberate budgetary decisions.

Your use of resources sends a message to staff, parents and community leaders as to what is most important and that you are serious about your role in making those decisions.

Enacting the budget is a crucial opportunity for school board members to step up to the plate. The phrase about putting your money where your mouth is may be a tired one, but it looms large in the board's efforts to ensure alignment.

Ensuring alignment also means you are willing to eliminate programs and positions that are not critical to achieving the district's goals. Cutting any program can be a political mine field for school boards, and this is particularly true when an unproductive program has powerful advocates. Such sacred cows must be held accountable for results that are consistent with the priorities of the school district. If they do not contribute, those resources can be realigned to meet the goals of the district. Alignment is particularly critical when budget reductions become necessary. Boards can only find alignment through decision-making that is driven by facts and focus, not by politics and perceptions.

HOW DO YOU SPEND YOUR MONEY AND YOUR TIME?

Let's look at this issue of resource allocation in more detail. Nothing conveys what is important to a school board more than the budget it adopts. You may tell staff and the public that accelerating reading skills in the early years is a top priority, but if more dollars are allocated for athletic equipment and relatively little money is allocated for reading instruction and teacher training in methods of reading instruction, it's obvious what the board thinks is really important. If your typical board meeting agenda devotes most of the time to routine business such as approval of proposed purchase agreements for school supplies, and almost no time for the things you and the system say you value, such as the reading program and other instructional priorities, the message to all involved will be clear: business as usual.

The ideal, of course, is that you and your board member colleagues will have determined, with appropriate public input, how you will spend your money and time to achieve the school system's vision and goals. It means that you have determined in advance how you will make budget decisions and you have communicated that process to the superintendent, staff, and community.

Community groups, employee organizations, and others have learned to exert political influence on the budget process. When money is tight, people run to defend their turf and protect themselves from cuts. When money is available for growth or improvement, they all come to get their piece of the increasing pie. The problem for you as a school board is that the arguments put forth are generally good ones. Everybody who comes to you believes that what they are proposing is good for kids and teachers. And, at some level, they are probably right.

Dealing with teacher unions and non-certified staff unions is one the most difficult and ongoing challenges the board will face. A lot of good research on work and motivation has been done over the years and many of the findings are instructive.. One of the things that researchers have learned about salary (and benefits) is that no matter what salary schedule is negotiated, it is never satisfying to staff in the long run. This year's raise, no matter how large, is next year's baseline. Salary is never a "satisfier." The next round of negotiation will result in even larger demands for compensation. No matter the agreed-upon increase, the cycle will repeat itself.

Certainly, teachers should be fairly paid. The point is to understand what salary and benefit increases can and cannot do. Salary and benefits are large chunks of the budget. Money that is spent on salary and benefits is not available for other use. Seeking to buy teacher satisfaction by giving "budget-buster" raises eliminates other choices.

One way of thinking about the issue is return on investment (ROI). In a competitive market, salaries have to be on par with comparable, neighboring districts and should attract and retain good teachers. Boards have to make calculations during negotiations as to what that means in dollars and cents, not an easy calculation to make. Whatever the decision turns out to be, the board should recognize that paying the highest salaries and improving benefits will not automatically result in improved student achievement. There is little if any credible research that would support such a conclusion.

School boards often find themselves caught in the middle. It is natural to want to be responsive to all parties and to do good things. The problem is that absent clear goals and priorities, the board may end up being whipsawed and give in to one request after another until the money is all spoken for. When decisions are made that way, focus is lost, and mission drift, the enemy of alignment, is inevitable. When the board holds to its goals and priorities and uses them to make budget and program decisions, the board is practicing alignment.

ALLOCATING STAFF IS AN ALIGNMENT ISSUE

Education is a people-intensive business. Negotiating salary and benefit schedules is just the beginning. The next challenge is determining how those human resources are allocated to enhance student performance. This process varies significantly from district to district. Some districts determine all staffing decisions at the district level using fixed formulae that have been set in place over time. Districts that favor this approach believe that it guarantees consistency and fairness. One reading teacher per school, one math specialist per school, and so forth. In fact, until recently this approach was considered the gold standard for equity.

However, this approach does not take into account the varying needs of students in different communities. Equality as traditionally defined does not guarantee equity. The needs of students vary widely based on socioeconomic and other factors, and the district has the responsibility to account for those differing needs when staff is allocated. Some districts have moved to a "weighted" formula approach that provides lower student/staff ratios in communities where the socioeconomic characteristics result in greater student need for enrichment and individual attention. Other districts have developed weighted formulae for determining equitable staffing and resource allocations based on individual student needs.

Whatever process your system uses, the school board should understand and agree to it. Absent that conversation, the process that is used may or may not support achieving the priorities you have established for student performance. It is equally important that stakeholders also are able to see how staff allocations support system goals and priorities.

When the board approves a staff allocation process/formula that is based on priorities and identified needs, it is practicing alignment. The only way for staff and parents to argue with the allocation process will be to disagree with the goals and priorities themselves, which is where the debate belongs.

HOW IS CURRICULUM ALIGNED AND WHAT IS THE BOARD'S ROLE?

Developing curriculum is the work of staff, but ensuring

that the curriculum supports the district's priorities for student achievement is part of the Key Work of School Boards.

When it comes to program issues, there are critical checkpoints and questions of which board members should be aware. After all, the curriculum is the lifeblood of school system programs. If the curriculum is not directly tied to the learning standards set by the district and the state, how can teachers and students be expected to achieve the desired performance results? Curricular congruency and alignment must begin with pre-kindergarten and continue through grade 12. The curriculum must be clearly sequenced pre-k-12 within each content area to make sure students are being taught what they are expected to know and be able to do at each grade level. The curriculum should be standards based, using both external and internal standards established at the local and state levels.

Many staff would have the board believe that approving the curriculum is job number one for the board. In fact, it is job two. Job one is to ask good alignment questions before approving curricula and program recommendations. Let's suppose the board is reviewing a proposal for a revised secondary mathematics program. In this case, the board would want to know the link between mathematics courses taught at the middle school and high school levels. The board might also want to understand what textbooks and technology are to be used to support instruction. These are only suggestive of the kinds of information that will help the board make better decisions with respect to curricula proposals.

Having a standards-based curriculum does not mean that the curriculum is a lock-step march for all students. To the contrary, the opportunities for students to accelerate should be clearly evident throughout the curriculum. Likewise, the curriculum must provide opportunities for struggling learners and accommodations for students with special needs in order to ensure that all students meet the standards. Instructional strategies and sample assessments based upon best practices and research should be included to support and inform teachers' work. The curriculum should serve as the framework and guide for the classroom teacher, but never preclude the teacher's own skills and adaptations to help students succeed.

HOW IS STAFF DEVELOPMENT ALIGNED?

It is ironic that educational institutions spend far less time and money on training their employees than their counterparts in the corporate world. Too many school districts view staff development as a fringe benefit that is made available when budgets are good and taken away during lean years. Even boards fall into this trap and neglect their own professional development, forgoing attending conferences and other professional development opportunities to set a good fiscal example.

How often are boards cowed by criticism from newspapers for attending conferences using public funds? Despite such flak, which in some communities is predictable, the board needs to set an example for staff and for the community by valuing and taking advantage of professional development activities at the state and national levels. They should report back to their communities what they learned and how it will be useful to them going forward. They need to put money in the budget for their own professional development up front and be willing to defend their actions when challenged by the naysayers. It is called leading by example.

When district training for staff is provided, it is either handled directly by the school district staff or by hiring outside presenters who meet with teachers, introduce new ideas, and move on to the next district to repeat the same process. The assumption is that teachers will be able to take what they heard back to their classrooms and implement it without further assistance. Study after study challenges the efficacy of this professional development model, but it is still the most prevalent approach. In many cases, districts also support advanced training for staff at institutions of higher education through tuition

reimbursement. The benefits to the district using this approach also are questionable at best.

The question of support for training, however, is not just one of quantity or even quality. The even larger challenge for school boards is to ensure that the training being provided will advance the priorities of the school district. In particular, boards need to understand how the training that is proposed will contribute to improving student achievement.

Consider this example: A school district decides that improving student achievement in science in elementary schools is a priority. One decision made by the board is that elementary teachers need more content expertise. As a consequence, the board doubles the number of science credits required for teachers in the district, and sets a deadline for current staff to meet the new requirement. At the same time, the district continues with its current set of course offerings for staff training, which does not include any additional science content courses. It also continues with a tuition reimbursement policy that is first come, first served. The district is spending time and money on training, but none of it supports the board's goal to enhance elementary teachers' scientific understanding. By realigning training to include more science content, the district not only would make better use of time and money, but it also would reinforce the message that elementary science achievement is a district priority.

The same argument could be made for other significant issues, such as technology training, providing for students with special needs, and fostering appreciation of cultural diversity. The capacity of staff development to be flexible and to adapt to the focus and direction of the school district is an essential element of alignment. The board needs to understand the types of training being offered and the proportion of that training that is clearly tied to district priorities. Training needs to support directly the results you seek.

HOW ARE OTHER RESOURCES ALIGNED?

The board also should understand and approve the processes used to determine the selection of textbooks, instructional materials, and technology. What part do these resources play in achieving the desired results? If, for example, technology is a major thrust of the school district, will there be equal access for all students? Teachers must be competent to integrate the use of technology throughout the instructional program. Even the facilities themselves should be aligned as renovations and other improvements made to support instruction.

In the end, alignment is most likely to occur when everyone is clear about the goals and works to achieve them. Alignment moves the district toward systemic approaches and away from random acts of improvement. The board's articulation to parents and community on the rationale for its decisions increases public understanding of the school system's priorities and community support.

WHAT WILL IT TAKE TO GET THERE?

Set up a process for reviewing board policies in light of current goals and priorities. An interesting exercise for any board is to open the policy and procedural manual produced by its district for the use of staff and community and read what it contains in light of the existing goals, priorities, and conditions. Often there are huge disconnects among these elements. Sometimes the federal or state laws change but never find their way into the policy manual. Often, too, policies are in place that are outdated and even contradictory to what the board and district are committed to doing. Another issue is whether in some cases a policy is needed at all. Even a cursory review of many district policy manuals also reveals confusion between policies and procedures. Generally, policies are intended to reflect what the district expects of its programs and staff. Procedures are generally the province of the superintendent and articulate how district policies are to be implemented. While the task of policy alignment and updating is daunting, your state school boards association is prepared to provide direct support in this important alignment issue.

SCHEDULE REGULAR WORK SESSIONS

Boards regularly meet in formal session to conduct district business as required by law. These sessions generally are designed to produce decisions and to receive reports and recommendations from the superintendent and staff. The formal nature and purpose of these meetings too often stifles legitimate discussion and debate that can help the board understand, clarify, and act with confidence as decision makers. One result can be decisions that are not well-aligned and that create mission drift because they are taken in isolation and without the benefit of careful board and staff deliberation. A wonderful tool for improving decision making and alignment is to schedule at least one work session per month in place of a second formal meeting. Work sessions are opportunities for the board to hear a variety of voices and perspectives on substantive programs and other issues. Frequently, these meetings are structured to permit folks to sit together around a table with the board and discuss current and future issues, laying the groundwork for future decisions that would take place at a formal meeting. One result is better decisions that are aligned with board goals and priorities and reflect broader consensus.

REQUIRE THAT ALL PROGRAMS REFLECT ALIGNMENT WITH EXISTING GOALS AND PRIORITIES

Keeping this requirement front and center enables the board to ask "big picture" questions about what is being proposed and how it supports program and student performance goals. It is also a great opportunity to identify the "sacred cows" that consume valuable resources but provide relatively little in terms of return on investment. It also sends an important message to the community that the board is serious about accountability and will examine each program and proposal on its merits and ability to contribute to the district's achievement of its vision.

REFLECT REGULARLY UPON YOUR OWN ACTIONS AND ALIGNMENT

If all of this seems too abstract, step back for a moment and reflect on what you as a board are saying is important as a school district and compare it to what you actually do. A great resource for making that comparison is the agendas for board meetings. Looking back over a year's worth of board agendas in terms of topics covered and time allocated can be very helpful in this exercise.

Ultimately, the board sets the example for alignment for the district. Alignment begins in the board room.

ALIGNMENT SELF ASSESSMENT Indicate the degree to which your board/district has achieved the following elements in aligning resources for improving student achievement

4	3	2	1
Fully Achieved	Mostly Achieved	Partially Achieved	Beginning to Achieve

4 3 2 1
We have established a specific and limited set of priorities for improving student achievement that give everyone in the district clear focus.

4 3 2 1
We make staffing and resource allocation decisions based on our student achievement priorities.

4 3 2 1
We ensure resource equity for schools by providing additional supports to schools in communities with higher needs.

4 3 2 1
We view the budget as the vehicle for accomplishing our priorities rather than simply as our spending plan.

4 3 2 1
We leverage resources within our budget to achieve our priorities.

4 3 2 1
We add or delete programs and initiatives based on analysis of data and district priorities.

4 3 2 1
We have no sacred cows within our budget.

4 3 2 1
Our curriculum and program initiatives are directly aligned to our student achievement priorities.

4 3 2 1
Our textbook, instructional materials, and technology selections are directed by our student achievement priorities.

4 3 2 1
Our staff training is designed exclusively to support our student achievement priorities.

4 3 2 1
All units in the district including all support services focus on their role in accomplishing the student achievement priorities.

4 3 2 1
As a board, the criteria we use to make all decisions are our student achievement priorities.

STAFF ALIGNMENT QUESTIONS THE SCHOOL BOARD SHOULD ASK ITSELF

- How do staff development efforts relate to student achievement goals and objectives?
- How do the qualifications of our teachers compare to those in districts with high student achievement?
- Do teachers have the skills to address the learning needs of students—at risk, special needs, and achieving?
- How are decisions about spending for professional development made?
- How are teachers involved in setting professional development objectives and establishing professional development programs?
- Do we know the kinds and costs of training that are purchased or are different accounting methods needed?
- How can teacher mentoring and collaboration be encouraged?

STAFF ALIGNMENT QUESTIONS THE SCHOOL BOARD SHOULD ASK THE SUPERINTENDENT AND STAFF

- What percentage of teachers is qualified to teach in their field of instruction?
- Does the quality of teachers vary from school to school and if so why?
- Are compensation rewards linked to obtaining professional development in the teacher's subject area?
- How are staff assignments made? Are they based on accountability and student needs?
- How are teachers evaluated to determine if they are teaching to the standards they and their students are held to?
- What needs to be done to improve the quality of teaching—changes to collective bargaining contracts, identification of research-based instructional practices, working with colleges and universities to ensure that new and veteran teachers are well prepared?
- What are our staff development priorities?

CURRICULUM AND TECHNOLOGY ALIGNMENT QUESTIONS THE SCHOOL BOARD SHOULD ASK ITSELF

- Is the curriculum aligned with state and district standards?
- How are the needs of at-risk, special needs, and accelerated students met?
- Are students encouraged to challenge themselves and to take challenging courses?
- Is technology incorporated into the curriculum to enhance student learning?
- Do teachers know how to effectively use technology?
- How do the board and school administrators use technology to improve decision-making?

CURRICULUM AND TECHNOLOGY ALIGNMENT QUESTIONS THE BOARD SHOULD ASK THE SUPERINTENDENT AND STAFF

- Are there enough adequately trained staff members to develop curriculum?
- Do teachers have the support and understanding they need to align instruction with curriculum?
- Are subject areas explored in-depth?
- Are textbooks and teaching materials aligned with standards and the curriculum?
- Are textbooks and other materials current?
- How are decisions about textbooks and learning materials made and do they take into consideration the treatment of subject matter to provide understanding and the acquisition of knowledge?
- Is technology distributed and used equitably by staff and students?
- How is technology integrated into the curriculum to enhance student achievement – higher order thinking and learning skills, student-centered learning, and collaboration and teamwork?

SUPPLEMENTAL SERVICES ALIGNMENT QUESTIONS THE SCHOOL BOARD SHOULD ASK ITSELF

- How do students' social and emotional needs impact achievement?
- Do we reach out to other organizations to ensure that student needs are met?
- What can we do to promote parent involvement in student learning?
- How can greater use be made of school facilities to promote achievement?

- Has the community been surveyed about the types of student and community services it wants and would support?

SUPPLEMENTAL SERVICES ALIGNMENT QUESTIONS THE BOARD SHOULD ASK THE SUPERINTENDENT
- Is there timely identification of students who are having difficulty meeting standards or who have social and emotional needs that affect their academic performance?
- How are we helping parents make good decisions about supplemental services required by NCLB?
- What assistance is available to such students—tutoring, summer school, remediation, transition classes, conflict resolution, youth programs?
- What services are available to students who are doing well—Advance Placement (AP) and other enrichment programs?
- How effective are parent involvement programs and how could they be improved?
- What organizations use district facilities and for what purposes?
- What community services are offered in schools—early childhood education, parenting classes, daycare?

BUDGET ALIGNMENT QUESTIONS THE SCHOOL BOARD SHOULD ASK ITSELF
- Are financial resources aligned with student achievement plans and priorities?
- Do operational plans and budgets provide the necessary programs and resources to promote student achievement?
- Are programs evaluated for effectiveness and are ineffective programs discontinued?
- Are funding decisions data-driven and research based?
- Do we have a good understanding of budget reports, procedures, regulations, and opportunities for flexibility?
- Is budget information provided to parents and other community members in an easy to understand format that conveys the relationships between budget items and student achievement initiatives?

BUDGET ALIGNMENT QUESTIONS THE BOARD SHOULD ASK THE SUPERINTENDENT AND STAFF
- What programs have we recently evaluated for effectiveness?
- How are programs evaluated for effectiveness/productivity—identification of inputs and outputs, controls for students' social and economic backgrounds, and links to student achievement?
- What value do programs add to the educational experience?
- What kinds of grants or technical assistance from government agencies are available to advance student achievement plans?
- What are future budget requirements and on what information are they based?
- How is the community engaged in the budget process?

PLANNING TEAM CONSIDERATIONS FOR DEVELOPING A PLAN FOR ALIGNMENT

1. What process will we use to review the following components of our program and budget to determine whether there is alignment with the established district priorities for student achievement?
   - Curriculum
   - Textbooks and instructional materials
   - Training
   - Staffing
   - Technology
   - Supplemental services for students with identified needs
   - System operations

2. Who are the key players in our community who will need to be involved in laying the groundwork for changing the way funds are allocated to programs? How can we get them involved early in this process?

3. What is a reasonable timeframe, given our budgeting process, to expect realignment to begin to occur?

ROLES OF THE BOARD AND THE SUPERINTENDENT IN RESOURCE ALIGNMENT	
THE SCHOOL BOARD	THE SUPERINTENDENT
1. Participates in training to better understand how alignment of the following resources is related to student success in meeting standards. • Staffing and personnel evaluations • Facilities • Funding • Curriculum and instruction • Assessment • Technology	1-A. Works with the board to increase its awareness and understanding on how aligning resources can pay off in increased student achievement. 1-B. Develops a process to ensure alignment of critical resources. 1-C. Provides annual update on the alignment process.
2. Assures curriculum alignment supports district priorities.	2-A. Assures development of curriculum directly tied to the learning standards set by the district and the state. 2-B. Provides staff with the support, resources, information, and training needed to align instruction with curriculum. 2-C. Reports to the board periodically and recommends additions or changes to ensure curriculum alignment.
3. Recognizes the authority of the superintendent to implement a district wide organizational structure that empowers staff to meet the needs of all students.	3-A. Aligns staff authority and responsibilities so that decisions for improving student achievement are made closest to the level of implementation. 3-B. Reports to the board on progress and recommends changes.
4. Approves and monitors policies to assure that students are encouraged to challenge themselves by taking higher level courses.	4-A. Recommends to the board policies and resources to encourage students to challenge themselves by taking higher-level courses. 4-B. Implements polices adopted by the board and makes sure that they are carried out equitably. 4-C. Provides the board with data on student enrollment and success in higher-level courses. 4-D. Conducts periodic review with the board to identify additional policies or review existing policies.
5. Considers student instructional, social and emotional needs when planning for improved student achievement.	5-A. Develops a process for timely identification of students who are having difficulty meeting standards or who have social and emotional needs that affect their academic performance. 5-B. Informs the board of assistance available to students including tutoring, summer school, remediation, transition classes, conflict resolution, etc. 5-C. Reports to the board the success or failure of programs and policies designed to help students meet student achievement goals. 5-D. Recommends changes or additions to programs and services based on student achievement data.

ROLES OF THE BOARD AND THE SUPERINTENDENT IN ACCOUNTABILITY

THE SCHOOL BOARD	THE SUPERINTENDENT
6. Assures staff development that will advance student achievement priorities of the district.	6-A. Assures a staff development program that supports student achievement priorities. 6-B. Ensures that teachers and instructional staff are involved in setting staff development objectives and programs. 6-C. Informs the board of staff development programs and their relationship to district student achievement priorities.
7. Approves the selection of textbooks and instructional materials that support instructional priorities.	7-A. Develops a process that involves staff and appropriate stakeholders in recommending textbooks and teaching materials that support standards and the district curriculum. 7-B. Recommends to the board textbooks and materials for adoption. 7-C. Monitors and keeps the board aware of the success/failure of textbooks and materials to support the reaching of student achievement goals.
8. Assures that technology is integrated into the curriculum to enhance student achievement	8-A. Develops a plan for the use and integration of technology into the curriculum to improve student achievement. 8-B. Ensures that technology is distributed and used equitably by staff and students. 8-C. Assures staff development and staff proficiency in the use of instructional technology. 8-D. Recommends changes to the technology plan as needed.
9. Assures school facilities that support student achievement goals.	9-A. Develops a long-range facilities plan to enhance the instructional program using a collaborative approach. 9-B. Works with staff and experts in school construction to determine costs and to prioritize projects. 9-C. Recommends prioritized facilities plan to the board with sources of funding. 9-D. Secures funding for projects. 9-E. Directs projects, assures timely completion of projects, and monitors expenditures. 9-F. Reports to the board periodically and recommends changes to the plan as needed.
10. Approves budget needs based on student achievement priorities.	10-A. Recommends allocation of resources based on school/district student achievement priorities. 10-B. Presents recommended budget to board based on resources needed to accomplish alignment. 10-C. Monitors expenditures and periodically updates board on status of the budget. 10-D. Assures effective communications explaining the district budget and the relationship it bears to student achievement goals.
11. Monitors progress of the district's instructional practices and programs as related to student achievement goals.	11-A. Assures school/district instructional strategies are in place to meet student achievement goals. 11-B. Recommends to the board programs that need to be added or deleted based on analysis of data and district priorities.
12. Ensures that the public understands the relationship between standards and curriculum.	12. Communicates, through the district's communications plan, the relationship between standards and curriculum.

POSSIBLE AGENDA ITEMS RELATING TO ALIGNMENT

A. Discussion of how our proposed operating budget is consistent with our goals and priorities

B. Discussion of external advisory group's report on our business operations procedures

C. Report and discussion of our district-wide staff development plan and how it relates to our goals and strategic plan

D. Report and discussion on our staff assignment strategies and procedures

E. Report and discussion of curriculum review process and adjustments relevant to our goals and our accountability data

F. Review of plans and evaluations of summer school and evening school programming

G. Report on process and results of program evaluations relative to our goals and priorities

PROFILE OF LEADERSHIP:
8. KENNEWICK SCHOOL DISTRICT

Data-driven decision-making is a relatively new trend in most school systems, as it largely has been prompted by school districts working to meet federal Adequate Yearly Progress (AYP) requirements and comparable state testing goals.

But in Washington's Kennewick School District, the focus on using data to direct instruction goes back 13 years. Kennewick has seen significant student achievement gains during that time, providing that you do not have to be in a large district with a deep administrative staff and ample resources to have a sophisticated data collection and analysis program.

Kennewick is a district of 15,000 students and 21 schools in southeastern Washington. More than half of the district's students are poor enough to be eligible for federal free lunches. In many ways, it is a largely typical American school system—which is why supporters find its progress so encouraging. Kennewick officials believe their systematic, data-focused approach to education reform is a plan that can be widely exported to schools across the nation.

SCHOOL BOARD LEADS INSTRUCTIONAL REFORM

It is easy for a school board to take a hands-off approach to student instruction, since most board members are not professional educators. Many school board members can become comfortable with letting the administration handle academics, while they focus on the financial and business aspects of running a school district.

But the Kennewick Board of Education did not accept that role, even in the mid-1990s. For years, board member Lynn Fielding had tried to get detailed data on high school student performance. Finally, after the district hired Paul Rosier as superintendent, Fielding got the information he wanted.

What he saw stunned him. Large numbers of students were flunking their ninth-grade classes, with many dropping out of school after falling behind. But at the time, no one was collecting accurate information on this problem, until Fielding spent an entire day poring over student records in the high school office.

"The situation was far worse than most people realized," he says. Other board members shared his concerns and, collectively, they decided to do something about it. They found a willing partner in Rosier. The superintendent was eager to work with the board in improving academic performance.

Fielding says the board's stability played a big role in the district's academic reform. Many members have served for a decade or longer and Rosier's tenure is at 13 years. In addition, the district made an effort to retain talented teachers and administrators. Fielding believes this level of stability absolutely has been a key in Kennewick's success.

"It was a perfect storm," Fielding says. "I really don't think it would've happened if we had different board or a different superintendent."

A FOCUS ON READING

What happened was that in 1995, the Kennewick Board of Education announced a daring goal: 90 percent of the district's students would read at grade level. That may sound commonplace in the era of No Child Left Behind, but in the mid-1990s, such a goal was considered outrageous, possibly even dangerous. Some employees felt they were being set up to fail.

What's more, Kennewick board members actually intended to pursue the 90 percent goal. Reading progress would be tracked and recorded using diagnostic tests.

CHAPTER 8

But despite the initial skepticism, board members felt that the district needed a concrete, objectively measurable goal. Otherwise, the effort to improve reading would go the way of so many other well-intentioned, but ineffective school reform plans.

Enthusiasm quickly built for the 90 percent goal. Board members met with principals and teachers to explain their reasoning and why dramatic improvement as necessary. The staff responded. "With elementary school teachers, there is a sense of 'Let's do the right thing,'" Fielding says.

Individual schools have significant leeway as to which reading programs to use and how to divvy up instruction time. However, three factors have emerged district wide:

1. A successful reading program must include skill-specific diagnostic measures. In Kennewick, students are given regular diagnostic tests, and instruction is focused on exactly the particular skills they need the most help in mastering. The approach is pinpoint, not scattershot, instruction.

2. There is no substitute for hard work. Traditionally, elementary school students have received between 60 and 80 minutes of reading instruction per day. But at many Kennewick schools, every student gets at least two hours of reading every day.

3. Small groups and individual instruction work. In many Kennewick schools, teacher assistants, administrators, and other staff members join in to teach reading during the daily reading block. Classes are dividing into small groups, with struggling students being grouped together in smaller numbers or even working one-on-one with an adult. The goal is to give every child as much individual attention as possible in a warm, welcoming setting.

Washington Elementary has been perhaps the district's greatest success story, having met the 90-percent-by-third-grade standard every year since 2000. The school's story was profiled in the 2007 book *Annual Growth for All Students, Catch-Up Growth For Those Who Are Behind*, co-authored by Fielding.

"We focus on direct, eyeball-to-eyeball instruction during the morning period, when students are fresh," says Dave Montague, Washington's veteran principal. "Direct instruction is becoming an art form in our school."

He says that when he was hired at Washington in the early 1980s, "I was hired to manage a building. Instructional leadership wasn't even on the radar screen....During the first decade I was principal, no one said, even once, 'Dave, show me data that proves that what you're doing is actually making a difference.'"

Now, Montague and his colleagues go over regular data reports, looking at the smallest indicators for determining instruction. Students are grouped and regrouped constantly to ensure they are receiving exactly the right instruction to meet their current needs. "That level of cooperation was unheard of a decade ago," Fielding says.

For his efforts, Montague was named 2005-06 Distinguished Principal of the Year for the State of Washington.

Other Kennewick schools also enjoyed strong reading gains shortly after the 90 percent initiative began. The number of students reaching grade level in third-grade reading shot up from 57 percent in 1995 to 74 percent in 1996. The district celebrated, perhaps a bit prematurely.

After a few years, improvement in third-grade reading hit a plateau, even dropping a couple of percentage points. Kennewick board members and district officials realized that they had gone as far as they could go with existing strategies. In order to make additional academic growth, new approaches were needed.

That meant district officials looked to the primary grades—kindergarten through second grade—for improvement. They made the decision to begin a dedicated effort to teach reading from the moment a child walked into school for the first day of kindergarten.

Fielding says that less than 10 percent of kindergartners could read and understand simple words and sentences. By 2006, 76 percent could read, based on a developmental reading assessment. Such a shift required a dramatic difference in how teachers approached educating younger students. Rather than look at kindergarten as a social transition grade, it became a time for academic instruction, particularly in reading.

A FORMULA FOR SUCCESS

If the average student needed more time on reading, Kennewick officials decided that struggling students needed even more time spent on reading.

In the Kennewick model, catching up on reading skills isn't the main goal for low-performing students—it's the only goal. Fielding says the outcomes for students who cannot adequately read are predictably tragic. And reading is required to do virtually any other subject, even math.

So in addition to the regular two-hour morning reading block, students who are behind grade level also get afternoon remediation in direct reading instruction. Some elementary students receive as much as four hours of reading, with little else on the schedule save recess and lunch.

That extra time is spent wisely; teachers don't reteach the morning lesson, they focus on the skills in which the student is deficient.

"If you don't know something, that's what you need to spend time on," Fielding says.

The school board also has ensured that its reading efforts are adequately funded, although Fielding says it has not required any real hardships. "A lot of what we've done is set priorities and say, 'Reading is the first priority,'" he says.

However, the board did allocate $500,000 to start up the reading effort, mostly for staff development. Fielding says the main benefit of that expenditure was to send a message to teachers and administrators that the board was taking the 90 percent goal seriously. The board's determination was reinforced by regular progress meetings.

In 2006, Kennewick did what some people said was impossible more than a decade earlier. According to state reading tests, 90 percent of the district's third-graders could read at or above grade level. Perhaps just as impressively, the lowest-performing school scored higher than the district average in 1995, when the 90 percent project began.

"When you look at the data, it is so predictable," Fielding says. "When you look at who is dropping out of high school, it's the kid who can't read."

9. CLIMATE AND CULTURE

Climate and *culture* often are used interchangeably. For purposes of this chapter, let's draw a distinction between them. Think of *culture* as the values and beliefs that shape the school district's behaviors, creating the conditions for teaching and learning. Those conditions are the *climate*. *Climate* is the product of *culture*.

School district leadership needs to pay close attention to the culture it exhibits and exemplifies, because this culture permeates the classrooms, directly affecting teaching and learning. School boards set policies and superintendents put procedures into place that influence the district's climate. This impact flows not only from the content of the policies and procedures, but also from the leadership behaviors and demeanors of the board and leadership staff as they carry out their responsibilities. The way they work with each other and the way they treat staff in the process sets a leadership tone that is a powerful influence on the behaviors and attitudes of staff and students.

Jim Collins writes about five levels of leadership that he has found in organizations. The highest is the Level 5 leader. Collins' studies of organizations that have gone from "Good to Great" define the characteristics of the Level 5 leader in creating a culture that leads to a climate of excellence. According to his research, "Level 5 leaders channel their ego needs away from themselves and into the larger goals of the company. It's not that Level 5 leaders have no ego or self-interest. Indeed, they are incredibly ambitious—but their ambition is first and foremost for the institution, not themselves."

Both the overall climate of a school and the specific learning environment of an individual classroom have enormous influence on student achievement. Students cannot learn in chaos, fear, or embarrassment. They must feel safe, and they need an orderly structure that is supportive of them. Every child deserves respect, encouragement, and opportunities to learn and grow. What are the elements of a productive climate, and how can school district leaders assess the climate of their district, their schools, and their classrooms? Where do they begin?

ENSURE A SAFE ENVIRONMENT FOR WORK AND LEARNING

A fundamental assumption of quality education is that children and staff have a safe place to learn and work. Recent events across the nation involving school shootings and killings have shocked and devastated us all. We no longer take for granted that our child's school is a safe haven. School leaders must take steps to ensure to the best of their ability that schools remain a safe place. How frequently these actions are taken should not be a function of the location of the school and the community served. No community is exempt, and no school board can overlook this responsibility. School boards need to develop policies and expect procedures that protect students and staff on school property. One way to strengthen such policies is by collaborating with other local or state authorities to legislate and implement laws that comprehensively and explicitly support school safety.

Some boards have "zero tolerance" policies regarding specified unsafe student behavior. The effectiveness of such policies is debatable because they end up criminalizing what some see as harmless acts (for example, a kindergartner suspended on the second day of school for having a tiny "GI Joe" gun). On the other hand, No Child Left Behind legislation required states to identify "persistently dangerous schools," and studies have shown that this requirement may have caused the underreporting of criminal activity. How can a school board create a balance between these extremes? What is the appropriate balance between an environment that is sufficiently controlled to be safe and yet sufficiently inviting to be attractive?

To start with, each board needs to have good data that describe the status of school climate. Board members need

CHAPTER 9

to seek and consider input and cooperation from the communities they serve. They need to listen carefully to the recommendations of safety and security experts. And they need to have policies in place to be sure that school officials work closely with the local public safety officials to assess, monitor, and ensure the safety of school buildings and grounds.

Creating and maintaining a safe environment is the necessary first step to a positive school climate, but it is not the only step. Climate is more than safety and order.

EXAMINE THE AVAILABLE DATA REFLECTIVE OF CLIMATE

Contrary to popular assumptions, not all climate-related data are "soft." Specific data can reveal much about the climate or the learning environment. One simple source of information is attendance data. Although school attendance is mandatory, patterns of student absence can be detected when comparisons are made among schools, races, genders, neighborhoods, and other student groups. Disparity in attendance may raise questions about the nature of the learning environment. Lower attendance rates may reflect the lack of factors that contribute to success, such as student motivation, parent support, teacher engagement, economic stability, and social comfort.

Suspensions and other disciplinary data are another source of information about school climate. These data should be analyzed for negative behavior patterns and opportunities for improvement. The analysis should examine the consistency of student treatment and of consequences for behavior. More important, data should be studied for cause-and-effect relationships. Determining the conditions that are most likely to generate disruptive or dangerous behaviors is the first step in preventing or reducing those conditions and, ultimately, altering the climate of the school. Alarming and tragic incidents of violence on campuses have shown the need for schools to be vigilant for students whose emotional needs put them and others at risk for violent behavior. A comprehensive student support program by staff professionally trained to recognize warning signs and to intervene early is important in creating a safe environment. Because public schools admit all school-age residents in the community, they must be prepared to deal with the full range of behaviors and emotional states that the community produces. Collaboration with community agencies is a necessity in ensuring that the most severe emotional problems in the community are addressed in a way that protects both the individual and the safety of the public. Boards should have in place the policies and the resources necessary to enable comprehensive prevention and early intervention for emotionally aberrant students.

EXAMINE THE CAPACITY TO MEET INDIVIDUAL NEEDS

With the increasing demands on schools in this era of accountability, public schools have the responsibility of bringing all students to proficiency. Students come to school with a wide range of aptitudes and interests, and bringing them all to a level of proficiency requires that those differences be addresses in the school program and in the classroom. In determining the proper educational "fit" for students, one size will not fit all, although all must be fit. A lockstep learning environment that attempts to herd all students to proficiency may lead to some students' falling out of step and not regaining their footing. The classroom teacher who recognizes and accommodates differences in student learning styles creates a nurturing learning environment. Such a learning environment allows each child to thrive and grow intellectually, socially, and emotionally. Accommodating differences entails a teaching model that uses data in a diagnostic way on a daily basis and instructional strategies and materials tailored to the individual student. Educational technology provides great opportunities for both the diagnoses and the prescriptions necessary to use this model.

Even in a classroom with a positive learning environment, some students may need supplemental or alternative settings in order to be successful. A school district's capacity to provide appropriate programs is another element of climate. School boards should know specifically where and how the district provides for students with special needs. Such students include but are not limited to students with disabilities, gifted and talented students, students with limited English proficiency, students in poverty, transient students, and students with interrupted learning. The capacity of a school district to identify needs and serve all students demonstrates the district's commitment to creating a caring climate and a positive learning environment.

SURVEY PARENTS AND STUDENTS TO DETERMINE SATISFACTION LEVELS

Much of school climate is a reflection of perceptions and feelings. If you really want to know what people feel about their schools, ask them. Some school districts have developed satisfaction surveys modeled after customer satisfaction surveys used in business. They view their parents as clients and seek to please them. Questions seek information about attitudes, perceptions, and personal opinions. They can then compare these perspectives to student achievement results to determine their correlation with success.

BUILD POSITIVE RELATIONSHIPS WITH AND AMONG STAFF

The staff members who work in the schools and the district office are important determinants of the climate in schools. A culture of relationships built on trust and mutual respect among staff members—and between staff and the board—helps to shape a workforce with strong commitment to the district and to its vision.

The climate in most organizations is set at the top. A positive climate results from a leadership culture that appreciates and publicly values the role that each person in the organization plays. One organizational strategy that places clear value on the individual is employee empowerment. Leaders who have faith in their own ability to select, train, and evaluate high-quality employees respect those employees with the following norm: Decisions are made as close as possible to the point of implementation. This means that the person doing the job can decide, within the policies and standards of the organization, the best way to do it. This empowerment is a powerful motivator because of the concurrent shared ownership of results. Empowered employees more actively share the organization's vision, and they bring to the job both commitment and creativity. They also welcome accountability.

The way board members interact with the leadership team sends a message about the value of staff in the eyes of the board. The way board members treat each other also influences the staff's perceptions and attitudes, with a consequent impact on workplace climate. Because that workplace is usually a school, board members' relationship skills and behaviors ultimately have an influence on the classroom environment and on student learning.

Board members also more directly influence climate and employee morale through carrying out such responsibilities as negotiating agreements or developing employee discipline policies. While these activities are to some degree inherently adversarial, many boards have developed relationships and procedures that include extensive input from staff, open dialogue on the issues, and decision-making processes that are based on established and mutually agreed-upon principles and policies. Certainly, boards at times must make difficult decisions that even a majority of employees may disagree with. If the board has built a long-term relationship of trust and follows its own openly developed procedures, it can retain the respect of employees and the positive climate that flows from that respect even in disagreement.

Positive relationships do not happen without a substantial and continued investment in skill building. For too long, teaching has been treated as a private act. Teachers develop wonderful skills in working with students but not with other teachers. First, they have few opportunities to do so, and the opportunities that they do have are scattered, fragmented, and squeezed into the hours before or after the students' day. Boards need to pay attention to staff development. Teachers need to understand the value of teamwork and mutual respect, develop the skills to practice them, and have the time to put those skills into action.

SURVEY STAFF TO DETERMINE SATISFACTION LEVELS

In the same manner as you examine attitudes of parents and students, you should survey staff to find out what they think and feel about their work and their work environment. The only way some boards gauge employee satisfaction is in communications with the employee organizations that represent them. While those interactions are integral to the running of a school district, additional information can be very helpful. School districts are organizations of intense human resources. What are the perceptions of the people who make up the organization? Do they share a sense of ownership for the shared vision? Are they proud of the work they do? Do they have ideas for improving that work? Are they proud of the organization and committed to its success? Gathering and analyzing such data can give district leaders a sense of the "state of the organization" as well as direction for change.

COMMUNICATE WITH THE MEDIA

Public confidence is another way of gauging school and district climate. Parents form their opinions based on first-hand experience with their child's school. In most communities, however, a great majority of the citizens do not have children currently enrolled in public schools. For these members of the community, their perspectives are primarily the result of second-hand information. A major source for that information is local media. School district leaders cannot control the media, nor should they try. A mistake that school leaders do make, however, is to ignore the media and to underestimate their influence on the broader community.

Tendencies to avoid media contacts are strongest when school leaders are dealing with bad news. If you have bad news, tell it quickly. Open communication from school boards and school leaders enhances the chance for including positive information along with bad news. In the absence of information from school leaders, reporters will seek other sources, usually within the organization. These sources may not have accurate information or they may bring a negative perspective. This then becomes the basis on which much of the public forms its perceptions of the schools. And, in the case of climate, perceptions can become reality.

MAKE SCHOOLS AN INVITING PLACE TO BE

Schools belong to the community. In many cases, the schools virtually define the community. However, schools are not always welcoming places for students or their parents. First impressions can be lasting. The message begins at the front door. Signs such as "No Visitors" or even "Visitors must report directly to the main office" set a cold tone for communities. Certainly, schools want all visitors to check into the office for security purposes. A sign that says, "Welcome. Please come first to the main office for a visitor pass or assistance," accomplishes the same security goal and extends an invitation at the same time.

The front desk of the main office is another measure of the climate of the school. Prompt attention to assist the visitor with a friendly smile and a helpful attitude reassures parents that their child's school is a positive environment. On the other hand, if individuals are made to wait and are treated abruptly or with indifference, they will be offended and concerned for their children.

The true measure of invitation extends beyond the first impressions. The role that parents and other community members are invited to play contributes greatly to the overall school climate. Traditional roles of baking cookies for school fund-raisers or other peripheral activities are not sufficient. Volunteering can be a rewarding and productive opportunity for community members, but many parents want more. They want to participate in planning and sharing responsibility for improving student achievement. In short, they want a seat at the table. Schools that build true partnerships with their parents build a shared positive climate.

CLIMATE SELF ASSESSMENT

Indicate the degree to which your board/district has achieved the following elements of climate for improving student achievement:

4	3	2	1
Fully Achieved	Mostly Achieved	Partially Achieved	Beginning to Achieve

4 3 2 1
We model the core values and beliefs of our shared vision in our work as a school board.

4 3 2 1
We provide a policy framework that gives clear direction and empowers the superintendent and staff to meet the student achievement goals.

4 3 2 1
We provide the superintendent and staff adequate resources to meet student achievement goals.

4 3 2 1
We align staff authority and responsibility so that decisions are made at the level closest to implementation.

4 3 2 1
We foster a culture that promotes the highest expectations for achievement for all students.

4 3 2 1
We create a climate that values and celebrates student achievement as the top priority of the district.

4 3 2 1
We encourage staff to risk failure as well as success as part of the continuing challenge to improve student achievement.

4 3 2 1
We encourage students to take risks by enrolling in more challenging courses.

4 3 2 1
We have clear policies that establish safe schools and promote orderly, positive learning environments.

4 3 2 1
We maintain school facilities that are designed and equipped to promote the highest student achievement for all students.

CLIMATE QUESTIONS THE SCHOOL BOARD SHOULD ASK ITSELF

- Do district policies allow for flexibility at the school and classroom levels? Does the school board avoid micromanagement?
- Does the district have the flexibility it needs to foster student achievement—are there state and federal regulations that hinder student achievement initiatives?
- Do we regularly make student achievement a part of our meeting agenda?
- Do the school board, administrators, and staff model mutual respect, professional behavior, and a commitment to continuous learning?
- Do school board policies hold staff and students to high behavioral standards? Are there clear and consistent consequences for those who violate policies?
- Is the school board a vocal advocate for student achievement issues among local, state, and federal policymakers?
- Are facilities adequate and designed to promote a sense of community—smaller schools, schools within schools?

CLIMATE QUESTIONS THE BOARD SHOULD ASK THE SUPERINTENDENT AND STAFF

- How is climate assessed?
- What do students, teachers, parents, and other community members think about the climate in district schools?
- Is data collected on student discipline incidents?
- What is being done to create a safe and positive learning environment?
- How are understanding, commitment, and accountability to others promoted?
- Do teachers have the time and resources to achieve standards?
- How do we recognize outstanding staff and student performance?
- What are the avenues for two-way communication and are they adequate?

PLANNING TEAM CONSIDERATIONS FOR A POSITIVE CLIMATE FOR STUDENT ACHIEVEMENT

1. How can we identify the data that are available to gauge climate in our schools?
2. How will we get feedback from key school district constituents regarding school climate?
3. What can we do to prepare our schools to respond to the feedback they get regarding climate?
4. How can we examine our capacity to serve special populations successfully?
5. How can we promote agreement on the ground rules for the way that our board and senior staff should interact with each other and with other staff?
6. How can we promote mentoring and induction programs for new staff, students, and parents to help develop a positive district-wide climate?
7. How can we assess whether we have positive communications with the media?

ROLES OF THE BOARD AND THE SUPERINTENDENT IN CLIMATE

THE SCHOOL BOARD	THE SUPERINTENDENT
1. Fosters a culture that supports the belief that all children can learn at higher levels in these ways. • Employing and supporting a superintendent who shares that philosophy • Developing and revising policies to reflect this philosophy	1-A. Develops a plan for recruiting and retaining qualified staff. 1-B. Assures employment of qualified staff. 1-C. Assures a staff evaluation process that supports student achievement goals. 1-D. Recommends assistance for staff not meeting evaluation criteria, followed by dismissal recommendations if necessary. 1-E. Develops and revises policies to meet student achievement goals and to assure recruitment and retention of qualified staff.
2. Approves and monitors programs designed to meet special instructional needs of students who are not meeting achievement goals or standards.	2-A. Recommends instructional programs or approaches for special instructional needs based on data and best practices. 2-B. Provides updates to the board on these special programs. 2-C. Institutes process for evaluation of programs and recommends needed changes to the board.
3. Provides adequate resources to meet student achievement goals through the budgeting process and monitors budget regularly.	3-A. Communicates with the board about resources needed to meet student achievement goals prior to development of the budget. 3-B. Develops budget based on student achievement goals and discussion with staff and key community groups. 3-C. Recommends budget to the board. 3-D. Reports monthly on implementation of budget and allocation of resources.
4. Recognizes and rewards staff and students for high academic achievement and high levels of improvement.	4-A. Develops and recommends to the board a plan for regular recognition of students and staff. 4-B. Carries out recognition programs.
5. Conducts all board meetings with student achievement as a clear focus.	5-A. Works with board chairman to develop a board agenda with a focus on student achievement. 5-B. Coordinates staff presentations for board meetings.
6. Models respect, professional behavior and a commitment to continuous learning. • With fellow board member • With superintendent and staff • With parents and students • With community	6. Models respect, professional behavior and a commitment to continuous learning. • With board members • With staff • With parents and students • With community

ROLES OF THE BOARD AND THE SUPERINTENDENT IN CLIMATE	
THE SCHOOL BOARD	THE SUPERINTENDENT
7. Serves as advocates for higher student achievement in the community and also at the state and federal levels.	7-A. Serves as an advocate for higher student achievement with staff and the community. 7-B. Works with board to provide information needed for understanding and communicating student achievement goals to the community. 7-C. Serves as an advocate for higher student achievement with state and federal officials.
8. Provides orientation for board candidates and for new board members on expectations for student achievement.	8. Works with the board to develop an orientation model for board candidates and new board members.
9. Assures periodic assessment of school climate throughout the district. • attendance data • discipline data • surveys of students, staff, parents • enrollment in higher level classes • staff turnover • student enrollment trends	9-A. Identifies and implements surveys or other means of assessing the school climate for high student achievement. 9-B. Collects, compiles and analyzes data related to school climate. 9-C. Reports periodically to the board on the results of school climate assessments and data trends and recommends changes. 9-D. Assures that appropriate changes are made. 9-E. Recommends additional policies or policy revisions.
10. Assures a safe and orderly learning environment in all schools.	10-A. Works with the board to develop appropriate policies and revise as needed. 10-B. Assures that actions are taken to implement board policies. 10-C. Reports periodically to the board on issues related to school safety. 10-D. Makes changes as necessary. 10-E. Makes recommendations for board action as indicated by need. 10-F. Collaborates with other community officials, organizations and groups to review and update district safety and emergency management plans. 10-G. Assures staff training on appropriate safety and emergency measures at each building.
11. Builds public support for higher student achievement and increases public trust of the district through formal and informal communication and through openness	11-A. Works with board, staff and community in an open, positive manner. 11-B. Implements district communication plan that ensures accurate information, regular channels for community involvement, and input and attention to customer services throughout the district. 11-C. Assures openness by district staff in relations with all stakeholders.

POSSIBLE AGENDA ITEMS RELATING TO CLIMATE

A. Review district's discipline policy along with a report on summary data on suspensions and expulsions disaggregated by race and gender.

B. Recognition ceremony for students and employees who achieve noteworthy success.

C. Discussion of board policy (do we have/need one?) and district practices regarding school climate surveys among parents, students, and staff members.

D. Report and review of induction and mentoring programs for new staff.

E. Report and analysis of success rates for retaining newly-hired teachers after one, three, and five years of service.

F. Report on school facilities and their adequacy for students and staff comfort and efficiency.

G. Discussion of district policy and practices regarding site-based decision-making.

H. Review of policies on community involvement and accessibility of school facilities for use by community groups.

I. Board members' self-analysis of their civility in working with staff and with each other.

PROFILE OF LEADERSHIP:
10. YORK COUNTY (VA.) SCHOOL DISTRICT

In education reform circles, data-driven decision-making often is seen as a tool to turn around struggling or underperforming districts. But Virginia's York County School District is proving that it can have a positive impact on already successful school systems, too.

The nearly 13,000-student suburban district in the Hampton Roads region has a number of demographic advantages. Employment is stable and strong, thanks to several large military bases in the Norfolk/Newport News/Hampton region. Many York County residents work either on the bases or for businesses that support the military. The county's median household income is nearly $70,000 and the poverty rate is only around 5 percent. Perhaps York County's biggest demographic challenge is in handling the large influx of new students, whose families are drawn by the region's good jobs and good schools.

But, like leaders in every school district in the country, York County's school board and superintendent have been feeling increased pressure to meet state and federal test score goals, particularly the Adequate Yearly Progress (AYP) targets mandated under the No Child Left Behind Act.

"The York County School District has historically utilized data to make instructional decisions," says Page Minter, chairman of the district's Board of Education. "However, data-driven decisions became more focused as Virginia's accountability program was implemented."

Beginning in 2002, the district began focusing on student-level data, as well as information at the school and district levels. In 2006, each school's individual improvement plan was rewritten to reflect an emphasis on data-driven decision-making. The results have been promising, Minter says, as the York County schools continue to trend upward.

A COMPREHENSIVE DATA ANALYSIS PROGRAM

Inertia is difficult to overcome in any school system. Established patterns of behavior are hard to break and expectations are difficult to change.

This can be particularly true in an already high-performing school system such as York County. The old adage, "If it ain't broke, don't fix it," will be brought up to counter any attempts to change the status quo.

But York County school leaders knew they needed to make improvements in order to meet the increasingly difficult demands of high-stakes accountability. They also felt that while most students were doing well, certain students or groups of students might be falling through the cracks.

District officials use benchmark tests to collect and evaluate student progress and regular intervals throughout the year. The benchmarks are aligned both with state standards as well as local curriculum expectations in reading, math, science, and social science/history. In 2008, the district made this benchmark data available online to educators.

But the district doesn't just collect the information—it uses it to drive classroom and school decisions. Data collected from the benchmark assessments are reviewed by administrators. The data reviews are guided by a rubric of questions. When concerns or questions are generated, additional information is collected.

Once information is collected, a dossier is created and reviewed by school officials, who then make recommendations for how best to proceed.

Minter says, "We are constantly disaggregating the data by school, by class and by individual student level to make specific changes to instruction, or on a division-wide level to develop and realign curriculum and to pace instruction."

This approach has led to a number of positive results. Test scores on the Standards of Learning, Virginia's annual stan-

CHAPTER 10

dardized tests, are increasing. In particular, the district has seen its lowest-performing subgroups and schools make considerable improvement.

In addition, more York County students are taking and passing Advanced Placement courses and tests at the high school level. And more minority students are taking the SAT, with scores increasing over time.

"However, we have ups and downs yearly and are constantly disaggregating the data by school, by class and by individual student level to make specific changes to instruction, or on a division-wide level to develop and realign curriculum and to pace instruction," Minter says.

The emphasis on data also has led the district to reconsider how it classifies students as "special needs." Several years ago, nearly 30 percent of the district's African-American students were classified as needing special education services. District officials examined the detailed data made available by the more sophisticated information collection systems and determined that minorities were being over-classified as special needs. Now, just 6 percent of African-Americans age 6 to 12 are in need of special education services.

Despite the community's prosperity, York County has a fairly high amount of residential turnover due to the number of people serving in the military. This type of mobility creates challenges for school districts to generate reliable data over time. But York County officials are working on ways to better track students as they move into and out of the district.

BOARD RELATIONSHIPS A KEY TO SUCCESS

So why exactly do the York County school board members have such a good relationship? Does it have to do with the personalities on the board? Is it a particular approach they take to governance? Is it something in the waters of coastal Virginia? Even the board members aren't completely able to explain what makes them such a good team.

But board member Barbara Haywood says it all begins simply with a willingness to work together. She says every board member comes to the table ready to collaborate and compromise. However, she and other board members note that this collaborative, cordial approach is a conscious decision and one that the board actively works to achieve. It is not something that happens by accident, they say.

"We are five different people, but we don't have any pre-set agendas when we come together," Haywood. "We are focused on student achievement and we have a good working relationship."

Board member Linda Meadows says people serve on the York County board for the right reasons. They aren't looking to use the board as a stepping stone to higher political office, she says. The York County board has experienced relatively little turnover, as board members tend to stick around for years. Minter, for example, is entering his 20th year of service on the board.

"We're not political," Meadows says. "We're focused on the York County School Division."

Board members extend that same approach to building relationships with the superintendent and staff.

Chief Academic Officer Lucia Sebastian came to York County in 1982 as a teacher. The school board then, she says, listened to teachers. "That approach has prevailed over time," she says, noting that staff members and teachers feel they can voice concerns to board members without fears of repercussions.

In 2008, the board hired Eric Williams to be the district's next superintendent. Again, the board valued relationship-building in its approach both to the hiring process and oversight of the new superintendent.

CHALLENGES REMAIN DESPITE SUCCESSES

Like many suburban communities, York County has plenty of professional parents who are active in their children's education and who hold the schools to high standards. While school district officials appreciate the support, this level of parent involvement can create its own set of problems.

"We live in a community where all parents believe their children are college-bound," Minter says. But he says that simply isn't a realistic expectation. Like many high-performing districts, he says the York County can do a better job of serving students who aren't headed for a traditional four-year college education.

"We're concerned about the kids who are getting lost in the cracks," Minter says. To help meet that need, the school board recently started an academy where students can earn Microsoft certification, which can help them get a well-paying job in the information technology industry. He also wants to improve the district's vocational offerings and promote awareness of these courses.

Another source of concern for board members is funding.

The York County School District continues to grow, meaning more money is needed, both for regular operating expenses and to build new facilities—the district currently is in the middle of a construction campaign. However, the board lacks its own taxing authority and depends on the county for its local budget. Every year, school board members clash with the county's Board of Supervisors over funding.

"We have had our share of struggles with our Board of Supervisors and I don't think that is going to end any time soon," Haywood says.

Minter says the county has been reluctant to give the board sufficient funds to increase teacher pay because the Board of Supervisors feels that York County is a desirable location to live and teachers will come even if pay isn't as high as in some of the surrounding counties. Not surprisingly, board members disagree with that sentiment.

The budget situation got even worse during the late 2008 economic downturn. The school board announced it would have to delay some of the scheduled construction projects because of funding shortfalls. In addition, a planned $525 bonus payment to teachers had to be cancelled.

Williams, the district's new superintendent, says his most important goal is taking the district's progress to the next level. He says the district has done a good job of getting more students and schools to meet a basic level of competency. Now, Williams says, it is time to focus on getting more schools and children to an exemplary level.

For example, the sixth-grade calendar was realigned for the 2008-09 school year to provide 135 more hours of math and language arts over the course of the year. Sixth grade is one of the "gateway grades" between elementary and middle school and a successful sixth-grade year can go a long way to ensuring a good start to middle school. The changes were made after teachers and school leaders analyzed data from the sixth-grade level and decided more emphasis needed to be placed on these core subjects.

Another point of emphasis has been on preparation for Advanced Placement exams. While noting that the York County schools have done a good job of both increasing participation and getting more students to pass the AP exams, Williams wants to see more students earn scores of 4 or 5 on the 5-point system.

"We want to push for excellence," Williams says. "We want to move beyond basic proficiency to excellence."

11. COLLABORATION AND COMMUNITY ENGAGEMENT

Community engagement is central to the school board's role. Governance in the age of public accountability cannot use the script, "We're the professionals; come listen to us and we'll tell you what you need to know." As the governors of the school district, board members come into office knowing that they represent the community that put them there. When they take on governance of large and complex organizations that comprise most school districts, board members can be consumed by routines and regalia and lose sight of the reasons they hold their office. Effective boards make deliberate, ongoing efforts to establish and maintain protocols and processes that actively seek the community's voice and enlist its commitment to the public schools. Seeking—and hearing—the community's voice and enlisting its support is an effective strategy for balancing competing interests and moving toward a productive consensus within the school system and in the wider community.

The most effective way to solve complex challenges is to bring multiple perspectives and experiences to bear through collaboration. Collaboration engenders ownership of the problem as well as the solution. Moreover, it brings richer resources and perspectives to the task. Educational leaders cannot hope to create and sustain high student performance working alone. In short, school boards and school district leaders must build networks of collaborative relationships that bring key stakeholders into the process of solving the challenges facing public education.

Building collaborative relationships, like every other challenging task, is easier to talk about than it is to accomplish. Often referred to as "an unnatural act performed by unconsenting adults," collaboration is difficult because it requires going beyond simply sharing knowledge and information. Moreover, it is more than a relationship that helps each party achieve its own goals. "The purpose of collaboration is to create a shared vision and joint strategies to address concerns that go beyond the purview of any particular party," write authors David Chrislip and Carl Larson.

Effective school boards long have recognized that the nature of public schooling's impact on the community gives everyone in that community an interest in the success of schools. While parents have an immediate interest in school quality and school operations, other community members also have a stake in the schools. This stake comes in the form of both the investments community members make through their taxes and the need they recognize for a well-educated cadre of graduates who will become contributing members of society.

School boards that involve the broader citizenry through effective community engagement activities have had great success in garnering broad support for necessary school funding, even in difficult financial times. Beyond the financial support that community engagement can generate, community collaboration brings into schools additional social, emotional, and experiential resources that can raise student achievement to heights unattainable by principals and teachers working alone.

WHO ARE THE NECESSARY PARTNERS IN COLLABORATION FOR STUDENT ACHIEVEMENT IN THE 21ST CENTURY?

PARENTS AS ESSENTIAL PARTNERS

Every school district recognizes the importance of supportive and involved parents. Two truisms are worth repeating in this context. The first is that the parent is the child's first teacher. The second is that it takes a community to educate each child. Parent engagement is core to effective collaboration between the school and the community. Parents need to feel that they have a meaningful role in the school, that their voices are heard, and that their input is valued. Significant long-term efforts to improve student achieve-

CHAPTER 11

ment cannot be sustained without parental understanding and support. When parents have high expectations for their children, those students are more likely to have high expectations for themselves and to act accordingly. Parents intensify the efficacy of the school's efforts with students when they understand what is happening and reinforce the importance of doing well. Parents who believe in the district's educational goals and performance standards become invaluable allies in the community-wide effort to support and improve the schools.

Building collaborative relationships with parents requires meaningful roles for them that go beyond helping in the media center, baking for cookie sales, and chaperoning field trips. Parents who assist with learning activities both at home and in the classroom, who tutor students in need of additional support, or who help prepare instructional materials contribute directly to increased student achievement.

The climate of public accountability demands greater parent involvement because it shines a light on the areas of need, and the urgency to improve. School districts that create pathways and provide support for parental involvement are tapping into the first essential resource for student success.

EXTERNAL PARTNERS

While every citizen in the community is a potential partner, successful school districts have made special efforts to build relationships with business and political leaders. Both of these potential partners have much to say about the resources and requirements that schools must meet, and both have a significant interest in school success.

BUSINESS LEADERS

Effective boards and superintendents encourage and welcome businesses' participation in school district initiatives such as standards setting, assessment, and accountability. The involvement of business leaders strengthens the systematic planning process advocated in the Key Work of School Boards because it adds both expertise and credibility.

While many board members are themselves successful business persons, they benefit from other perspectives on district issues and processes. These boards ask community volunteers to review school system operations in which the volunteers have particular expertise, and they pay attention to their feedback. One of the principles of effective communication is not to ask for feedback unless you are prepared to act on it. Nothing is more frustrating or alienating to citizens than to be asked to participate and then be ignored. Acting on the advice and recommendation of stakeholders does not always require agreement, but it does require an open analysis and public discussion of the recommendations received. Moreover, it requires openness on the part of the school district to re-examine its practices in light of the expert advice of business partners committed to collaboration.

Other members of the community in professions such as medicine, law, agriculture, manufacturing, ranching, construction trades, and other field of expertise all have something to offer to school districts. Opening the doors and meeting rooms of the school system and providing all community members an opportunity to participate bring an enormous wealth of experiences and perspectives that can improve both the quality of school operations and the richness of students' learning experiences.

The rising tide of awareness of the need to strengthen STEM (Science, Technology, Engineering, and Math) programs as part of 21st century learning creates a perfect opportunity to engage the business community in school improvement and program enhancement. Every aspect of our contemporary world of work requires employees with high levels of quantitative skills and technical understanding, combined with an ability to solve problems, think creatively, communicate effectively, and work collaboratively. School districts find it hard to keep up with this rapidly changing technical world. They can benefit enormously from developing relationships with local businesses and industry, which in turn have a stake in preparing students who, either immediately or after some post-secondary education, will enter this dynamic and demanding job market. As schools and businesses collaborate, each learns more about the realities that the other faces, and both add their expertise to developing proficient students.

POLITICAL LEADERS

School board members in most communities are elected, but other locally elected leaders also have a strong interest and a large stake in schools. Some of these political leaders control the resources needed by schools, while others have the power through legislation to impact school operations. Successful school boards build collaborative relationships with these political leaders through a variety of strategies. They also keep the political leaders well informed about school system policy and program changes and about the academic improvements that result.

Preserving local school district autonomy starts with demonstrating to those who would preempt it that the local school board and staff are doing an effective job in meeting high standards of student performance. State legislatures—frequently with prodding from the governor and the public—have been active in promoting public accountability. School boards should make every effort to keep legislators informed about their initiatives to raise student achievement. Political leaders never should be forced to rely on the media to learn about the public schools in their jurisdictions. An effective school board makes it its business to communicate regularly and thoroughly with all political leaders associated with its district. It keeps them informed about accountability data that it collects, and it invites them in for discussions and analyses of district strengths and areas for improvement. Smart school districts also recognize publicly the political leaders who contribute to school success through effective legislation and through providing needed resources.

HOW DOES A BOARD OF EDUCATION BUILD COLLABORATIVE RELATIONSHIPS?

There is no formula or ready prescription, but the following practical steps can jump-start and strengthen the process:

Communication. Community engagement starts with two-way communication. School district leadership has the essential responsibility of informing parents and other community members about issues and events in the public schools. As leaders, you must hear what the parents and community think, especially when they disagree with you. Two-way communications is the basis for working together to identify and address issues. Look at your district's communications mechanisms, including your website, and your press releases, newsletters, and other publications. Do they communicate clear, straight stories about what your district's accomplishments and challenges are? Are they clearly written and illustrated with specific events and anecdotes to make their point? Readers will remember (and retell) a story about student success or teacher heroism much more so than they will recite a policy or analyze a data table. Does your communication invite community reaction and input? Engaging your community starts with keeping them well-informed and aware that their reactions and feedback are welcomed.

Consider restructuring your board meeting. Community engagement is very difficult when a board meeting agenda appears to be an impenetrable monolith of official actions and tightly timed discussions about predetermined topics. A "Community Comments" time slot with limitations on how much time each speaker is allocated may be an effective meetings management strategy, but it is not a very engaging way to bring in the community members as partners. Driven by the twin necessities of involving the community and carrying out its business in an orderly fashion, some boards use the strategy of dividing their work into two types of meetings. One is a "work session" that involves a wide-ranging discussion of major issues, with explicit invitations to community representatives to participate as appropriate, and with the clear understanding that no action is taken at such meetings. The second meeting is the typical "business meeting," during which formal action is taken on whatever business the board has before it. The business meeting can be considerably shorter because it focuses on action discussed and debated in the work session, during which there was extensive dialogue with staff and community. While board members may choose to give brief rationale statements for their decisions at the business meeting, longer deliberations should be limited to the work session when community dialogue is part of the process.

Model collaboration for others. Values in an organization define what we will and will not do to accomplish our goals and the way we treat others and ourselves in the process. Collaborative relationships are based on trust and the respectful treatment of others. Boards must model the kind of relationships that they seek to build with and among others. The way you run your meetings sends clear signals about how you value collaboration. A board of education that behaves contentiously and provincially is not likely to build credibility among community leaders or enlist them as partners in their schools' success.

It is important to try to "see" your board's actions and your own from the perspective of what the audience sees. Regular board retreats with skilled facilitators, such as those that your state school board association can provide or recommend, will help the board focus on its own working relationships, ground rules, and values. When the discussion gets off track, redirect your attention to your vision and goals. In the last analysis, what you *do* is far more persuasive than what you *say*.

Invest in the process of relationship building. Collaborative relationships rarely emerge spontaneously except in emergencies. Because we assume, incorrectly, that relationships can be established just by putting people together in groups to solve problems and carry out tasks, we almost never spend time thinking about the group itself, and how a group of individuals becomes an effective team. Collaborative relationships must be cultivated in a deliberate and purposeful way.

Team-building activities conducted by skilled trainers help a group build trust and develop effective ways of communicating together. For boards, retreats and other reflective sessions can serve this purpose. An orientation program for new board members, usually available from your state association, is essential for helping new members see themselves as joining an effective team with a shared vision, not as entering a political poker game with the goal of winning as much as they can.

Invite others to the table. Many citizens feel alienated from the schools because they have no children in the schools, they have heard negative things about the schools, or they have not had positive experiences themselves. Many of these same individuals are community leaders and influence the opinions of others. The board needs to find ways to bring these persons to the table to engage them in discussions about the schools and enlist them in helping to craft a vision for the future. Being invited to the table does not mean being invited to testify or react to proposals already on the table. Being invited to the table means being enlisted to help solve complex challenges, the most immediate being how to assure excellence and equity in student achievement.

Focus on the things that unite rather than those that divide. Building collaborative relationships requires finding common ground and creating opportunities to work together to accomplish mutually beneficial goals. In the last analysis, if we make time for dialogue and exploration, we will find that we agree more than we disagree. Too often, we spend most of our time focusing on areas of disagreement, thereby giving up valuable opportunities to collaborate and solve mutual problems. Finding common ground often requires reframing an issue. For example, the demands of public accountability challenge local boards to focus as never before on student achievement. A significant body of research confirms what most of us believe intuitively: When it comes to student achievement, teacher quality is the key. Skilled teachers consistently lead students to higher levels of achievement. Poor teachers have a negative impact that can last for several years of a student's schooling. What would happen if boards and teachers came together and worked collaboratively to develop plans for improving student achievement? Instead of seeing teachers as the problem, boards would be reaching out to teachers and enabling them to be part of the solution. Instead of fixing the blame, the board would be fixing the problem.

Collaborative relationships require time and attention to cultivate and maintain. School boards that seek consciously to build such relationships by inviting others to the table, investing in the process of reflection and skill building, and modeling what it expects of others can lead from a position of extraordinary strength.

Collaboration and Community Engagement Self Assessment—Indicate the degree to which your board/district has achieved the following elements of collaborative relationships and community engagement for improving student achievement

4	3	2	1
Fully Achieved	Mostly Achieved	Partially Achieved	Beginning to Achieve

4 3 2 1
We understand that collaboration begins with us.

4 3 2 1
We treat each other, the superintendent, staff, students, parents and community members with respect.

4 3 2 1
We take time to reflect on and improve our own internal and external relationships.

4 3 2 1
We view our communication with staff and the community as a two-way process.

4 3 2 1
We have policies and practices in place to encourage parents to be active partners in their children's education.

4 3 2 1
We encourage parents to share responsibility for the success of schools and students in pursuit of the common good.

4 3 2 1
We provide opportunities for community input into key actions of the board.

4 3 2 1
Our priorities and student performance standards reflect community needs and interests.

4 3 2 1
We build partnership with the business community and others that promote high student achievement as the top priority.

4 3 2 1
We support staff efforts to build collaborative relationships with other agencies (e.g., social services, police, juvenile justice) to provide child and family centered services.

4 3 2 1
We recognize, as a board, that our leadership responsibilities extend beyond the district to included state and national issues.

4 3 2 1
We communicate regularly with elected officials to ensure that public schools are and continue to be a top priority.

COLLABORATION QUESTIONS THE SCHOOL BOARD SHOULD ASK ITSELF

- Do we provide leadership and take an active role in establishing collaborative relationships?
- What alliances and collaborations would most advance student achievement goals and objectives (e.g., teachers, teacher unions, social service agencies, colleges and universities, businesses)?
- What other steps can we take to foster and sustain collaborative relationships?
- What are appropriate levels of stakeholder involvement?
- Is the community engaged in student achievement plans and initiatives at the district and school levels (e.g., surveys, forums, meetings, committees, school-based management councils)?
- Is the community well informed about the district's vision, achievements, challenges, and plans for improvement?

COLLABORATION QUESTIONS THE BOARD SHOULD ASK THE SUPERINTENDENT AND STAFF

- What collaborative initiatives are currently in place, what are their purposes, and who are the participants?
- What efforts are made to collaborate with groups with whom the district differs?
- Is there adequate outreach to various government agencies, education associations, and universities to keep current on education issues?
- How many outreach and student achievement initiatives are scheduled regularly on the district's events calendar?
- How does the district relate to the media?
- How are collaborative and engagement initiatives managed (e.g., definition of appropriate roles, responsibilities, expectations, decision making parameters)?

PLANNING TEAM CONSIDERATIONS FOR DEVELOPING A PLAN FOR COLLABORATION

1. How can we identify the key persons in our community with whom the board and superintendent should strive to collaborate?

2. Are there potential business partners in our community whom we should involve in the process of building collaboration? What can we do about it?

3. How can we seek out non-traditional partners with whom to collaborate within our district?

4. How can we determine which political leaders are most favorable to our district and recognize their efforts on behalf of students?

5. How do we build relationships and awareness with political leaders who are not supportive of our schools?

6. How can we build on what our teachers already do to create partnerships in the community that enrich the instructional program?

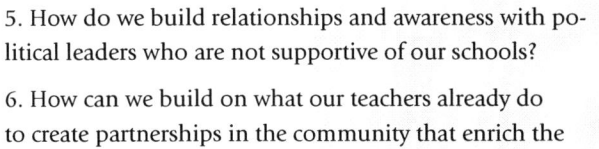

ROLES OF THE BOARD AND THE SUPERINTENDENT IN COLLABORATION

THE SCHOOL BOARD	THE SUPERINTENDENT
1. Fosters collaborative relationships as a board philosophy • Strategic planning • Community vision • Instructional improvements	1-A. Follows a collaborative approach in working with the board. 1-B. Encourages the board and staff to involve key stakeholders in appropriate decision making both at the district and at the school level.
2. Approves and periodically reviews a district plan to build collaborative relationships with key stakeholders at all levels based on gaining support for student achievement as the district's top priority.	2-A. Recommends to the board a plan to build these collaborative relationships, leads a periodic review of progress and implements agreed-to strategies for improved relationships. 2-B. Keeps the board and others informed about the district's progress and solicits appropriate input for areas of concern.
3. Models collaboration and trust.	3-A. Works with the board to determine a process for a periodic review of the leadership team's relationship and vision. 3-B. Implements changes recommended through the periodic review.
4. Advocates district positions on educational issues with legislators and other state and local political leaders and keeps abreast of other state and national issues.	4. Assists the board in its advocacy efforts with public officials by arranging meetings, providing needed data and information and scheduling other activities as needed.
5. Advocates student achievement as a top community priority.	5-A. Provides data and relevant materials to assist the board in its advocacy role. 5-B. Teams with board members to speak to groups within the community.
6. Assures a climate of open communications at board meetings and throughout the district.	6-A. Assures a climate of open communications, both internally and externally. 6-B. Recommends additional policies or policy revisions.
7. Provides funding and resources for collaborative efforts.	7. Presents budget recommendations needed to support collaborative efforts and initiatives.

POSSIBLE AGENDA ITEMS RELATING TO COLLABORATION

A. Policies and outreach effort to promote collaboration with local businesses that support the instructional program and provide outside review and advice regarding district business and operational practices.

B. Policy and outreach efforts to enlist parent involvement in instructional programs and the success of students.

C. Joint meetings with locally-elected officials to review school successes and priorities for improvement..

D. Meetings with community leaders—civic, political, religious—for feedback about schools and discussion of avenues for collaboration on mutual goals.

E. Emerging legislative issues, both state and national, and our district's advocacy efforts in collaboration with our state association and NSBA.

F. District and school-based efforts to include elected officials in recognition events for school, students, and staff.

G. District policy and practices to cooperate with the media.

12. CONTINUOUS IMPROVEMENT

Continuous improvement is in the first instance a habit of the mind, a way of thinking that focuses on doing whatever it is we are doing better. The term itself has become almost commonplace, but the concept itself is far from that. In fact a number of misconceptions about continuous improvement can get in the way of practicing it.

First of all, continuous improvement is not synonymous with total quality management, usually referred to as TQM. They are related, but they are not the same. TQM refers primarily to techniques or tools that can be used to analyze problems and generate possible solutions. Flow charting a process is one example. The flow chart helps clarify steps in a process and the relationships among them. There are many other such tools that are useful when they are well understood and employed correctly. It is important to make the distinction between tools to help us think and the actual thinking itself. At one point in the quality management movement, TQM tools assumed an almost faddish status. In too many workplaces, people found themselves being asked to use such tools without proper grounding just because they were in fashion. Consequently, for many, TQM became an exercise in futility. There are still people who will want to run and hide when they hear the term TQM being used.

Continuous improvement is not merely a set of management tools. Rather it is a different approach to managing. Certainly, there are analytical tools and skills that can help organizations practice continuous improvement when they are used properly and kept in perspective. But analytical tools, no matter how simple or complicated, do not make decisions for us. They can help us make good decisions, but they are not a substitute for judgment.

No organization should consider itself to be a continuous improvement organization merely because it follows the principles and uses the tools associated with TQM. Organizations that practice continuous improvement in effect learn early on that establishing a culture is more important than the tools used. That culture is constantly seeking better and more efficient ways to operate. Continuous improvement brings a different perspective to an organization and to how it works. Continuous improvement essentially is a habit of the mind.

How many of you have heard individuals comment that change is not simply a matter of "talking the talk." To realize lasting and significant change one must also "walk the walk." Let's face it. It is easier to talk than to walk. If it were not, change and improvement would be easy to accomplish, but we all know that it is not.

While there is truth to this aphorism, from a continuous improvement perspective, it leaves out an important step. In an organization that is thinking in terms of continuous improvement the first step, for sure, is to talk the talk. Articulate what is needed to achieve a better result. But the intermediate step, the continuous improvement step is to "talk the walk." Try ideas on by thinking about them, talking about them, and projecting what would happen if they were implemented. In this intermediate step, analytical tools can be very useful. When we have talked the walk in the way suggested here, then we are ready to walk the walk. And even then, there will be missteps and false starts and mistakes. Eventually, if we have really done our homework, we can be successful.

Throughout the process, the board plays an important role in helping staff members by supporting their efforts and proposals. The board also needs to take a critical review of its own processes to be sure that they are in alignment with the system's direction. The board needs to monitor its own talk and walk.

In a very real sense, continuous improvement begins when we teach ourselves to think about what we are doing in very deliberate ways. "Routine drives out planning" is a

CHAPTER 12

maxim in administrative circles. After all, we like routines and there are good reasons why we do. Most of the routines that we follow help us do the things that need to be done, both on a personal and a professional level. They generally serve our purposes well or they would not become part of our routines. Over time we become more and more comfortable doing them. If you doubt the efficacy of this maxim, look back over several months of your board's meeting agendas and check all items that you would consider to be routine. The proportion of routine items may surprise you. You may need to ask yourself if the comfort of your routine is driving out your responsibility to think and plan.

Not only does routine drive out planning, it also can drive out improvement. Routines unchecked become ruts. Stable can easily become stagnant. Margaret Wheatley, one of the more insightful students of modern organizations, once observed that, in this day and age, any organization that finds itself in a stable state is near death. Her statement is a powerful reminder of the challenges we face in keeping schools and schooling relevant in a rapidly changing world.

The antidote is to begin thinking about the present in future terms. What works well today almost certainly will work less well in the future. It is the conundrum we all face. As Joel Barker points out, our past success in no way guarantees our future success. In fact, our tendency to cling to what has worked is often what blinds us to the present and the future, and leaves us bewildered about what to do in the face of new realities.

The advent of the calculator as an inexpensive and indispensable tool in mathematics and science instruction is a case in point. Not too many years ago, the notion that students could use calculators in class when working on complex mathematical formulas was resisted by most mathematics and science teachers. The transition for many was very difficult and they raised the specter of students not being able to do basic calculations in traditional ways and becoming mathematically illiterate. One excellent science teacher who embraced calculators early also insisted that his students learn first to use a slide rule—only then were they allowed to use a calculator. Not long ago, on tests like the SAT, students were not permitted to use calculators. Some school boards, with the support of parents, established policies forbidding the use of calculators in the classroom. Today, calculators, as well as computers, are commonplace in mathematics and science classrooms, allowing students to complete far more complex operations than they ever could have done with pencil and paper.

From another perspective, the advent of the calculator itself is illustrative of the process of continuous improvement. The early models that some of us still remember were large, unwieldy, slow, and expensive. Today, calculators are tiny, fast, ubiquitous, and cheap, and perform complex calculations that would cause the early developers of electronic calculators to marvel. That evolution did not happen overnight but reflects continuous improvement of the technology needed to produce better and less expensive calculators.

Almost everyone has heard the cliché, "If it ain't broke, don't fix it." If that observation is seen through the lens of continuous improvement, it would have to be rewritten as follows, "When it ain't broke is the time to fix it." While the grammar may be suspect, this statement does capture an important idea: Waiting until something breaks to fix it is usually too late. The key is thinking, always thinking, about what we do and about how we might do it better.

Anyone who has purchased a new car understands how rapidly technology is changing automobiles. Most of us spent the greater part of our time during the purchase period dickering about the price. Now a growing number of consumers use online sites to get accurate information about car costs and dealer markups. They arrive at the showroom having figured out pretty much what they will have to pay. Taking possession of the car, however, is now the more complicated piece. Cars come with a bewildering array of features, and it can take as much as an hour for the salesperson to explain what is available and how each works.

What is happening to automobiles is a perfect example of continuous improvement that is occurring all around us. None of us is naive enough to believe that all of the changes in new cares have been added solely for altruistic reasons. In reality, at least one automobile manufacturer included each of these options on one of its models and created new benchmarks for its competitors. Competition can drive improvement.

The idea of competition is challenging for public education. Competition traditionally has been limited to contests among students, usually between athletic teams. The idea of competition among schools and districts based on student achievement results is a new reality for educational leaders. The idea of comparing one district to another, one school to another, one classroom to another has been resisted and often labeled as unfair. Such resistance is grounded in the tradition in education that comparison must result in winners and losers. If one team wins, the other loses. If some students are in the top 10 percent of the graduating class, others are not. If some students are accepted to a college, others are rejected. By contrast, the concept of continuous improvement does not require someone to fail in order for others to succeed. If an organization embraces the culture of continuous improvement, they understand there is much to be learned from competitors that can improve not only their own organization but also the overall business.

In education we do not spend nearly as much time as we should seeking out best practices and using them as benchmarks for improving teacher, student, and school performance. Boards need to be asking the superintendent and staff to identify comparable schools systems that are performing better and use that information to set reasonable progress goals for their own system by drawing on the experiences of others. When we stop thinking about comparison in terms of winners and losers, we begin to see comparison as the driver of continuous improvement. When we believe in the culture of continuous improvement, we can embrace the core belief that all children can succeed. We can deliver in the mission of quality public education.

Continuous improvement thrives on good information in the school setting as elsewhere. School systems that are data driven are constantly seeking benchmarks by which to measure what they do and how well they do it. Data that is accurate and timely constitutes the feedback loop that empowers the board and staff to refine, strengthen, modify, and/or eliminate existing programs and practices—in short, make important and lasting improvements.

Because they are data driven, the board and staff will need metrics for determining whether a new program or process is getting better results. Continuous improvement requires that attention be given at each critical juncture to what data will be needed and how and when it will be used when changes are in the offing. Staff will need data that help them assess progress and make midcourse corrections based on their initial experiences. The board will need longitudinal data to determine whether the changes that have been proposed and implemented are getting the desired results. At the outset, boards need to ask three key questions of themselves and of staff:

1. What data do we need?
2. How should the data be displayed to help us understand what is happening?
3. Do we have the capacity to collect it?

The latter question is often the one that is most difficult to answer in the affirmative, because many school systems do not have data information systems in place that can provide timely and accurate data for staff and for the board. Remember, the objective of continuous improvement is to find better, more efficient and effective ways to work. Without good data, reaching conclusions about value added by a new practice or procedure will be very difficult to do. In the final chapter of this book we will have much more to say about building the information foundation that is critical to continuous improvement.

Continuous improvement is about doing our work more efficiently and effectively. It is a rigorous process. It is not "change for change's sake." It is about changing because we need to change. As human beings we are programmed with the capacity to see new possibilities and to invent better ways of getting to our destination. That capacity, in our time, has created an information revolution that is dramatically changing the way we work and communicate. As school leaders we must understand those changes and rethink the way the board carries out its mission.

For example, many boards and school districts now are using Web-based programs to perform many important functions rather than investing in expensive hardware and software. One example is Internet companies that provide paperless (read Web-based) board meetings that reduce paper production and give the public access online to board agendas and accompanying materials. The developer of one such program, which began in 2002, reported that the original program has been updated, upgraded, and customized to respond to individual board and school district needs well over 500 times in a six year period. In this new Web-based environment, customizing for individual clients and the pursuit of continuous improvement are fundamental to doing business.

One of the most urgent challenges facing boards of education is creating an organizational culture that values continuous improvement and encourages experimentation and innovation. The mind set of continuous improvement is to question, examine, revise, refine, and revisit. When it works well it is inclusive. It transcends hierarchical boundaries and positional authority. It looks for insight wherever and whenever it can be found.

Implicit in all that we have said here is the notion that continuous improvement is a journey, not a final destination. It is not something you finish. Improvements can be made to any process, if there is the will to do it. Continuous improvement, when it becomes part of the culture of the school system, is the feedback loop that keeps on giving.

WHAT WILL IT TAKE TO GET THERE?

Model continuous improvement as a board. Seek to improve the way the board does business. Pause frequently to reflect on public meetings and other activities and try to make them better. Ask for feedback from staff and others about ways to improve meetings and other functions of the board. Many groups use a process known as plus/delta to get feedback group members. Essentially, members are asked two questions and their answers are recorded and posted using newsprint or other means. The first question is, "What did you like about the meeting?" The second is, "What could we do differently to make future meetings better?" Responses to the second question must begin with a verb so that the feedback can be acted upon. For example, a person might say in response to the second question: "Provide background materials in advance so that members will be better prepared for the discussion."

Adopt a customer focus. For many educators, the notion of customer applied to students, parents, and others is alien and offensive. It has an air of commercialism about it that is contrary to the educators' world view. In this context, however, adopting a customer focus means understanding what we do and for whom we do it. Rich Harwood, a pioneer thinker about the future viability of our democratic institutions, bridles at the commercial notion of customer when it is applied to public institutions. He would argue, and we would agree, that parents and all community members are citizens first. They are not simply customers of the schools or any other public institution in their communities and nation. They are custodians, owners, and keepers of the flame. They are owners in the sense of being responsible for the institutions that serve the public good. Our democracy is very much predicated on citizen involvement and on local government and public agencies. If, he argues, we forget our role as citizens and begin to see our institutions as designed to serve our personal and particular needs, as a nation, we are in deep, serious trouble. In this instance, adopting a customer focus means fostering community engagement and broadening the dialogue about the place of public schools in our society. Certainly, when we are serious about community engagement, we also are striving to listen to our citizens and respond to their feedback about how to make schools work even better than they do now.

Make decisions based on the data. All of us have preconceived notions about what is effective and about how things should be done. Continuous improvement requires stepping back and reconsidering those preconceived notions if the data do not support them. Mary Parker Follett, a pioneer in organizational development and management theory, was fond of saying that decisions should be made not on the basis of who is right, but what is right. Of course, some issues have philosophical or ethical overtones that override process considerations. More often than is healthy, however, the real driver of decisions is past practices (the way things have always been done) and political considerations. We need to move away from politics and past practices to critical reflection that is data based. When something is not working, boards need to stop authorizing it. When something is working, boards need to challenge staff to build on that success and reward them for doing so.

Require that all programs—existing and new—have built-in data requirements. In countless ways, at budget time and throughout the year, the board makes decisions about whether a given program should stay, go, or be modified. It is critical, therefore, that the board establishes up front what data will be collected for its review and when it will be needed. Doing so—asking the right questions at the right time—also sends a powerful message to staff about the way that the board will make decisions. As important, the board may find that the district does not have the capacity to provide the needed data in formats that are useful to the board and staff.

If that is the case, the board may need to authorize the resources, materiel and human, needed to create that capacity. An exciting alternative to building capacity in-house by purchasing hardware and software and hiring staff to manage them is now available through the Internet, or what we call Web-based services. Districts can contract with service providers who can provide data storage and management systems, electronic board meetings, parental and community communication systems, and so forth, for very modest costs. It is an alternative that more and more school systems are taking advantage of.

Foster open communication and invite feedback. Information is the lifeblood of continuous improvement. A climate in which open communication is valued allows people to think outside of the box and share different perspectives without fear of reprisal. Dialogue is different from discussion. Dialogue invites differing perspectives and the open exploration of ideas; discussion aims at analysis and closure. Many boards now are transforming one of their monthly meetings into a work session during which substantive issues can be openly discussed without any attempt to make policy or other decisions reserved for formal meeting agendas. Staff and other experts are invited to the table to share their perspectives and insights. When those issues finally do come to the board at a formal meeting for discussion and action, the results more often than not are better decisions and greater consensus.

Celebrate evidence of improvement and reward those who are responsible for it. It is very easy to turn continuous improvement from a positive to a negative. Continuous improvement is about enlisting others to use their talents and experience to create a better school system and learning environment for children. When the efforts of those who create improvements are not recognized and rewarded, continuous improvement can rapidly give way to a kind of perpetual crankiness. When that happens, staff and others will view the board's questions and focus as negative, and they will respond accordingly.

Promote continuous improvement as an integral part of every policy and decision. Ask the question, "How can we do this even better?" publicly and often. Make others aware that the board is every bit as serious about finding even better ways to do the things the system is doing well as it is to improve things that the system is not doing well.

In summary, continuous improvement is not just a process; it is an attitude that must be cultivated and reinforced. It is preoccupied with quality and recognizes and rewards those who produce it. Continuous improvement creates school systems that are constantly adapting, striving to become what Peter Senge calls "learning organizations." That is, organizations that are so attuned to their environment and their clients that they are anticipating needed changes and improvements and making them before a crisis occurs. In the Information Age, any organization that is content with where it is and what it is doing presently almost certainly will fall behind. Continuous improvement is the antidote to that kind of complacency.

The rapid pace of change in our times is exponential and it is increasingly difficult not only to keep up but also to sort through the array of options and new capacities in terms of their utility, short term and long term. We cannot escape our times, and we should not try. The information revolution is changing the way students communicate, think, and learn, and we must seek to understand and respond effectively to those changes and to their learning needs. The path forward is through continuous improvement.

Continuous Improvement Self Assessment—Indicate the degree to which your board/district has achieved the following elements of continuous improvement for improving student achievement

4	3	2	1
Fully Achieved	Mostly Achieved	Partially Achieved	Beginning to Achieve

4 3 2 1
Our board and staff have been trained on the principles and tools of continuous improvement.

4 3 2 1
We have developed a culture that promotes quality as among the first considerations.

4 3 2 1
We manage by facts and our decisions are data-driven.

4 3 2 1
We focus on our customers and clients in designing and delivering our services.

4 3 2 1
We practice problem solving, prevention and intervention rather than reaction to promote student success .

4 3 2 1
We inculcate problem solving and risk taking to move beyond incremental improvement.

4 3 2 1
We use strategic planning to focus and drive our decisions and strategies for achieving our priorities.

4 3 2 1
We practice bench making with other school districts and businesses.

4 3 2 1
We treat all stakeholders with respect.

4 3 2 1
We practice constancy of purpose.

CONTINUOUS IMPROVEMENT QUESTIONS THE SCHOOL BOARD SHOULD ASK ITSELF

- Do we clearly communicate that we are committed to continuous improvement?
- Is continuous improvement built into planning processes?
- Are the programs and initiatives being assessed linked to short and long-term strategic objectives?
- Is there community participation in continuous improvement discussions and plan reviews?
- Do we focus on solutions to problems instead of blaming?
- Are adjustments made and resources reallocated in a timely manner?
- Do school board members, administrators, teachers, and other staff need continuous improvement training?

CONTINUOUS IMPROVEMENT QUESTIONS THE BOARD SHOULD ASK THE SUPERINTENDENT AND STAFF

- How often are program reviews conducted?
- What measures and indicators are used to provide feedback on achievement initiatives?
- How are assessments used to adjust curriculum and instruction?
- How are findings reported to the staff and public? Do they have the information they need and in an understandable format for informed discussion?
- Can data be disaggregated to help discover solutions to problems?
- What is being done to create a customer focus?

PLANNING TEAM CONSIDERATIONS FOR DEVELOPING A PLAN FOR CONTINUOUS IMPROVEMENT

1. What will our board need to create an ongoing program of board development, planning, and team building?

2. What are the resources in our community that we can draw upon to help us begin to develop a culture of continuous improvement?

3. What can we do to help the staff in our district become eager to participate in a continuous improvement process?

4. Does our district promote risk-taking? Does it reward individual and group efforts to promote student achievement? If not, what steps will be necessary to make these things happen?

ROLES OF THE BOARD AND THE SUPERINTENDENT IN CONTINUOUS IMPROVEMENT	
THE SCHOOL BOARD	THE SUPERINTENDENT
1. Follows a regular process to review student achievement data to ensure continuous improvement.	1-A. Recommends to the board a process for continuous improvement. 1-B. Sets and reviews benchmarks and performance indicators that demonstrate student progress related to the district's strategic plan and standards. 1-C. Provides clear analysis of relevant data related to student achievement. 1-D. Seeks input from professional staff on changes needed to strengthen instructional programs. 1-E. Recommends changes to instructional program indicated by data and staff input.
2. Takes part in training on principles of continuous improvement including use of data and customer focus.	2-A. Schedules training on principles of continuous improvement and participates with the board. 2-B. Assures ongoing training for all employees on principles of continuous improvement. 2-C. Assures professional development to build understanding of information provided by data and to encourage staff participation in needed changes.
3. Participates in work sessions to better understand needed changes in curriculum and instruction based on related data.	3-A. Presents information to the board on needed curriculum/instruction changes. 3-B. Explains data to support recommended changes.
4. Provides funding for continuous improvement.	4-A. Reviews curriculum and instruction plans and costs as part of the board's budget planning. 4-B. Presents budget recommendations to the board on resources needed for continuous improvement
5. Adopts board policies that support continuous improvement.	5-A. Recommends policies needed to support continuous improvement efforts. 5-B. Conducts periodic review with the board to identify additional policies needed or to revise existing ones.
6. Supports publicly and communicates the value of continuous improvement to the community.	6-A. Communicates the process and results of the district's continuous improvement efforts to key stakeholders as part of the district's communications plan. 6-B. Communicates both proposed and approved curriculum and instruction changes to stakeholders affected, such as students, staff, and parents.

POSSIBLE AGENDA ITEMS RELATING TO CONTINUOUS IMPROVEMENT

A. Review and discussion of benchmark data our district uses to assess its progress.

B. Quarterly report by staff on progress and measures in implementation of the district's strategic plan.

C. Report and discussion of district's staff development plans for continuous improvement process training.

D. Quarterly report and discussion of key indicators of progress on student achievement.

E. Yearly report and discussion not only of budget priorities but also of activities to be eliminated, with data to justify decisions.

F. Board retreat with senior staff for self-evaluation of board operations and effectiveness.

G. Discussion and planning for board development activities, including participation in state association meetings and NSBA activities.

13. PUTTING IT ALL TOGETHER—BECOMING AN INFORMATION AGE BOARD OF EDUCATION

Our world rapidly changed from the Industrial Age of the 20th century to the Information Age of the 21st century. Dramatic shifts in how we work, how we live, and how we learn continue occurring daily. Public education is not immune to these developments. In fact, the access to information and the exponentially increased capacity to report and analyze data is transforming how we work with our constituents. The public demands the reporting of student results. External groups analyze and interpret the performances of students. Schools and districts are rated and compared. Others outside public education are developing models for determining return on investment similar to business metrics. School district actions and the results of these actions are under constant scrutiny. The public expects and demands the same level of access to information that they take for granted in other areas of their lives.

Public institutions are undergoing dramatic transformations. If we examine how many school districts operate, we might find that the tradition of political influence and public perceptions have guided most decisions. These practices were understandable when board members had little or no access to solid data and facts. In today's Information Age, however, lack of access to data is inexcusable. Consequently, board members need to revisit how they make their decisions and, more importantly, how they evaluate the results of those decisions.

The Key Work components are grounded in the assumption that decision making in the organization is based on facts, not perceptions and politics. Accountability, alignment and continuous improvement in particular are dependent upon timely and robust information. School boards cannot be reluctant to invest resources in their information systems. Neither can they refuse to learn how to use data to guide their decision making. Building an information foundation is essential to achieving the Key Work of improving student achievement.

WE MUST BUILD A STRONG INFORMATION FOUNDATION

What does that mean? What is an information foundation, and why do we need one? How do we build one for our district? What steps should board members take to make this happen?

It is not necessary to be a statistical genius or computer whiz in order to make data-driven decisions. In fact, the purpose of a strong information foundation is to make data available quickly and easily, and in user-friendly formats. Data should be easy to interpret and easy to explain to others. With state test data being made available to the community through various public websites, parents and others are doing their own analyses and drawing their own conclusions about the success of schools. School districts must have the capacity to analyze and present their own data efficiently and effectively. They must be able to use the facts to tell their story.

ASK YOURSELVES THE FOLLOWING QUESTIONS:

- Do we receive data that is timely?
- Is the data provided in a user-friendly format?
- Do we discuss the data openly?
- Do we use the data to inform our decisions?
- Do we gather evidence to determine whether our policies are being implemented?
- Do we gather evidence about the impact of our policy decisions?
- Do we have the infrastructure in place to store, access, analyze, and report all the data we need to guide our decision making?

CHAPTER 13

Few school boards can answer *yes* to all these questions. Many may not answer *yes* to most of them. The accountability requirements of No Child Left Behind (NCLB) have changed how school boards and school district leaders must react in a data-laden environment. Having a purposeful and effective data structure for school districts is neither a luxury nor an option. Building an information foundation is essential for survival in this era of public accountability. Understanding how to use this information foundation to guide and review decision making is at the core of being accountable.

WHAT DATA BASICS SHOULD BOARDS KNOW IN ORDER TO BUILD AN INFORMATION FOUNDATION?

Remember that a picture is worth a thousand words. Board members already receive pages and pages of data each year, and NCLB is no doubt increasing the data load. Poring through reams of tables and number charts can be confusing and frustrating. Data should be represented in graphic format whenever possible. Graphs make comparisons more immediately evident. There are multiple types of graphs and charts, each with its own purpose and information. Board members should become familiar not only with the simpler types of chart, such as bar graphs, column graphs, and pie charts, but also with the more sophisticated types, such as stacked columns, scatter plots, and box-and-whisker plots. Because these forms are being used on many of the public data sites, it is important that board members be comfortable with interpreting them and using them to inform their decisions.

Use color to inform. A consistent use of color can provide instant information for board members, staff, and the public. The traffic light is a good example. Green always stands for go; yellow, caution; and red, stop. We can use the same technique for student achievement. Green represents proficient; yellow, partially proficient; and red, not proficient. We can add blue to represent advanced proficiency. Depending on the number of performance levels being reported, more or fewer colors may be used following the spectrum of the rainbow. In this spectrum model, green should always serve as the anchor, indicating proficiency in meeting the standard. Any color above green on the spectrum would represent exceeding the standard. Colors below green on the spectrum represent failure to meet standard with red always indicating high risk or lowest performance. Once colors are used consistently, colored graphs and charts allow for instant interpretation by anyone.

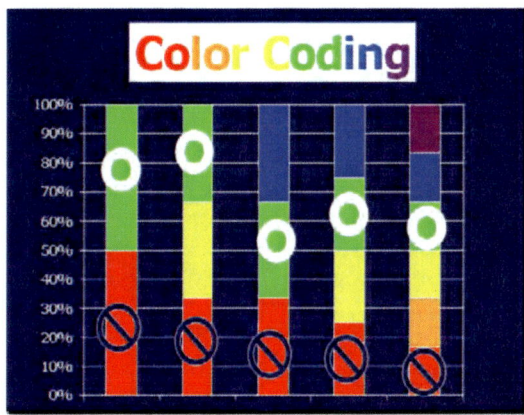

Use distribution models. Charts that simply show the number of students who met the standard or the percentage of students who are proficient do not tell the whole story. Average scores also provide less information than boards require for making good decisions. Distribution models such as stacked columns and scatter plots let board members know what proportion of students are at the various proficiency levels. They inform the board about student progress and track growth performance in a value-added model. All of these pieces of information are needed for boards to understand the direction of student performance and the effects of targeted strategies and interventions. As boards respond to the accountability push for Adequate Yearly Progress (AYP) as defined in NCLB, being able to gather this evidence is critical to changing direction to improve student achievement.

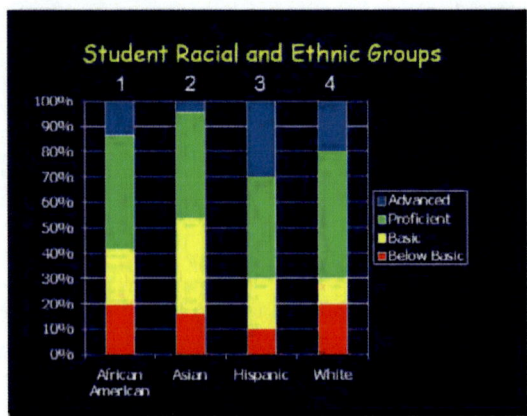

100 PERCENT STACKED COLUMN

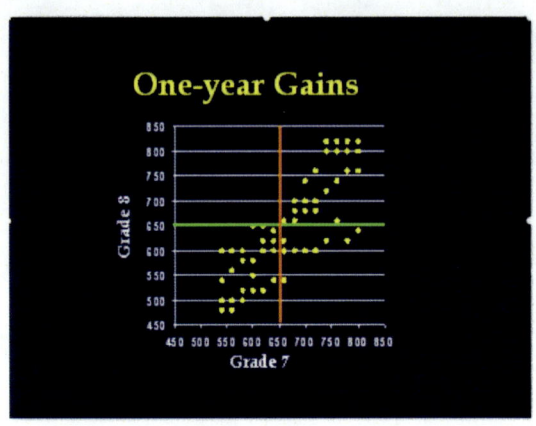

SCATTER PLOT

Disaggregate all data. Many school districts have been disaggregating student data by gender and race or ethnicity for years. Others have not. NCLB requires accountability for four student subgroups: economically disadvantaged students, those with limited English proficiency, students with disabilities, and racial or ethnic groups. Each subgroup must meet the standard along with the total population. School districts must monitor progress and provide interventions for each subgroup in order to meet AYP. To avoid cumbersome recalculation of data to meet NCLB requirements, all district data should be automatically disaggregated using the NCLB categories when the data is first collected and each time it is reported.

HOW DO WE MANAGE DATA OVERLOAD? HOW DO WE FIND FOCUS?

Use guiding questions. No matter how much data school districts and school board members receive and no matter what type of data it is, we can approach the analysis of the data by using a consistent set of guiding questions. There are three questions we always want to be able to answer, and all three start with the same phrase: 1) How are we doing compared to the standard? 2) How are we doing compared to ourselves? 3) How are we doing compared to others? These three questions represent multiple perspectives in viewing the same data. Each question plays its own role. All three perspectives are needed before boards and district leaders make changes or determine what is working and what is not.

1. How are we doing compared to the standard? Sometimes there is no standard against which we can compare a specific piece of data. More often than not, however, some standard does exist. That standard may be set at the state level, the district level, the school level, even the classroom level. Comparing our data against the standard tells us how close we are to meeting established goals and gives us a measure of *proficiency*. Comparison to a standard is usually the first step in examining data, but it does not give us enough information to make good decisions and set directions for the future. The standards may be too easy or too hard or based on rules that do not apply to our population. At best, using only standards to assess progress gives us an incomplete picture of the quality of the education our schools provide. At worst, it misleads us about our effectiveness. Standards are essential, but they are not enough.

2. How are we doing compared to ourselves? This is another way of asking what our trends are over time. Are we improving, declining, or flat-lining? This is our measure of growth and improvement. Accountability models that do not consider growth and improvement will penalize those students and teachers who start behind and have far to go to reach the standard. Comparing our data to ourselves gives us our measure of *progress*. These measures have become critical to Adequate Yearly Progress, the accountability model in NCLB. We must always consider not only where we are compared to standards, but also where we have been. By examining our improvement trends, we can predict the likelihood of achieving our ultimate goal of proficiency.

3. How are we doing compared to others? This last comparison is sometimes frowned upon as raising too much competition in the drive for learning. Teachers are reluctant to have their students' results compared to those of other teachers for fear that teacher effectiveness and pay for performance will be driving forces in measuring educational quality. Teachers also may be reluctant to take on high-risk students for fear their performance will be compared to that of other students. Fairer models exist for making comparisons among students, schools, and districts, taking into account similarity of student populations, for example, as well as growth from similar starting points in student learning. These models are frequently called value-added models. The best reason to compare ourselves to others is the opportunity to learn from others and improve our own effectiveness. This type of comparison is at the heart of the continuous improvement organization. Comparison to others should never be for praise or punishment. Rather, comparison should be for the purpose of learning and improving our work.

WHO SHOULD HAVE ACCESS TO THE DATA?

This is a complex question. It is important to be an open and transparent organization. As stewards of a public institution, we have an obligation to inform the public. At the same time, we deal with individual students and adults for whom we must protect confidentiality. That is why building a solid information foundation with a variety of accountability and reporting models is essential. As reporting and analysis tools become more sophisticated, we are developing models for analyzing our data that allow us to inform and monitor our decision-making but protect the privacy of the individuals behind the models.

If a school district does not yet have access to these more sophisticated tools, district leaders must use good judgment and common sense in terms of who has access to what data. There is a delicate balance. The data should be analyzed to a sufficiently discrete level for the board and district leadership to determine specific actions for improvement. At the same time, public reporting cannot in any way identify the performance of individual teachers or students. School boards should not have access to that level of information under normal circumstances. They should count on the professionals to examine the discrete data and provide appropriate group data together with trend information to help the board make the necessary policy decisions and set district initiatives.

Beyond the data required for public accountability, the school board should expect the development of an internal data-collection infrastructure. Such a structure raises the same questions about access. Certainly, each teacher should have access to all data available for his or her students. Traditionally, most teachers kept their own records of student progress, which they may have shared with the principal but seldom with other teachers. As we move into a standards-based educational environment, schools are adopting a team approach in which teachers share strategies and student results in order to plan interventions and monitor progress toward mastery. Schools that have developed this collaborative approach to teaching and learning share their data openly as a basis for making informed decisions rather than to reward or punish students or teachers. These schools have already discovered the value of continuous improvement as a means to their desired end of improved student achievement.

The principal must have access to all student data in the school. The data must be made available in a timely manner, with the capacity to group student results by the accountability categories in NCLB as well as by teachers. Principals who are effective instructional leaders are "data junkies" when it comes to monitoring student progress. They verify for themselves whether students are mastering the required learning standards. They direct interventions for students who fall behind, and they monitor with their teachers the effects of various instructional strategies.

The school board has a tremendous responsibility to see that teachers, principals, and district leaders have timely access to well-defined data collected locally in a consistent and organized manner. The purpose of the data is to inform the ongoing decision making that directs the district's instructional program. The data are only as good as their capacity to predict readiness for the high-stakes state assessments for NCLB compliance.

HOW DO WE DETERMINE THE EFFECTIVENESS OF OUR DECISIONS?

School boards make hundreds of decisions yearly. Some are basic operational decisions. Others concern policies and procedures that can change the direction of the district. It is critical that boards monitor the effectiveness of their decision-making, especially at the policy and governance level. What evidence can be gathered and where do we begin? Some school boards pass policies or establish initiatives without ever looking back. Future policies are introduced without reference to past successes or failures. Each policy develops in a vacuum, and change is unrelated to seeking improvement. Other school boards attempt to determine the results of policies but are not always clear how to proceed.

Gathering the appropriate evidence is often quite difficult.

Determining the success of an initiative or policy requires answering two fundamental questions. One of the questions is obvious, "Did it work?" That is really the second question. The less obvious (but necessary) first question is, "Did we do what we said we would do?"

Did we do what we said we would do? How do boards know that their policies are being fully implemented? Many simply assume that passing a policy makes it so. Others trust the word of the staff. The board has a responsibility to expect clear evidence that implementation has been carried out. This evidence should be provided not only for the district as a whole, but also for each individual school. The type of evidence that will be gathered should be determined and agreed on before the policy is implemented. That way, the expectations are clear up front, and the staff isn't being asked to provide confirming data after the fact.

It is not unusual to find that implementation is uneven from school to school. In fact, the larger the school district, the more opportunities for inequalities. An initiative that has not been correctly implemented cannot be fairly evaluated. The first measure in program evaluation is to establish that the program was implemented as designed. Fidelity of implementation is a necessary first step to determine the true effectiveness of any strategy. By answering the question "Did we do what we said we would do?" school boards verify fidelity of implementation and set the stage to answer the next question, "Did it work?"

Did it work? This second question can only be answered after the first has been resolved. And this question may be even more difficult to decide. The key to determining whether something worked depends on having clearly defined criteria for success. As Chapter 1 counseled, begin with the end in mind. What results did we anticipate when we passed the policy? What does success look like? How long do we expect it will take for the policy to have the intended impact? What evidence will we gather to determine success or lack thereof? Can we have partial success? What will we do if we don't achieve the desired results?

HOW CAN WE DETERMINE RETURN ON INVESTMENT (ROI)?

ROI, a term used frequently in the private sector, stands for return on investment. Is our investment paying off for us? Investment for school boards includes not only the dollar figure spent on a program or an initiative, but also the human effort required. When examining achievement results, it is critical to disaggregate data beyond the standard NCLB groups and disaggregate by interventions and treatments provided for groups of students. Do different interventions yield different results? What are their costs? Is there correlation between cost and results? This is how boards begin to determine what works and what does not together with what it costs. Cost should not be restricted to dollars and cents. Cost estimates should also include the difficulty of implementation for the people involved. It is easy to disregard the human factor when computing costs because teachers and administrators are not paid overtime. Nevertheless, if excessive outside time or training are required for successful implementation of a program, this needs to be acknowledged when deciding ROI. There are ROI analysis models that address the issues facing school districts. Once again, the capacity of school boards to collect meaningful data is critical. They can determine ROI on behalf of their students. Assessing ROI in the era of public accountability is a major governance responsibility.

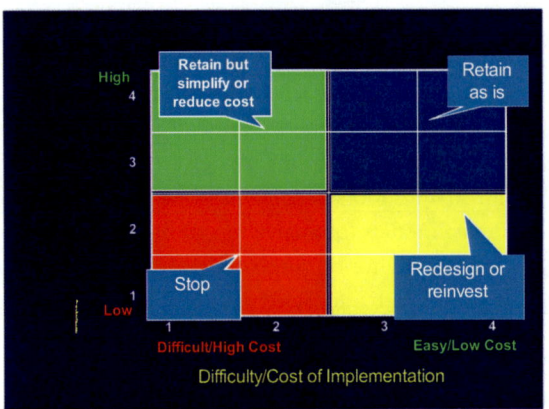

WHAT ABOUT SYSTEM PROCESSES AND OPERATIONS?

The discussion so far has focused on decisions that directly affect student results because improving student achievement is, ultimately, the key responsibility of school boards. That is not to imply that accountability begins and ends at the classroom door. Business operations, systems processes, personnel practices, facility maintenance, transportation, food services, and other support functions that make a school district work well can and should be viewed through the accountability lens. Gathering data that reflects the effectiveness of decisions about system processes and operations is a key part of school district accountability.

Ask yourselves the following process questions:
- How do we know that the processes we are using are as effective as we would like?

- What data can we gather?
- What factors contribute to the success or lack of success in the final measure of student results?
- What factors do we control as a board?
- How do those factors correlate with the end results?
- What can we change?
- How will we monitor the impact of those changes?
- How do we spend our money?
- How do we allocate our staff?
- How do we invest in our human resources through staff development and training?
- What is our ROI?

School districts have a business side, and the board must try to make those business systems as cost effective and as service oriented as possible. Use the same guiding questions and approach to analysis that we have discussed in looking at student achievement. But the most important question to raise is: How do the various investments in the operations of the school system pay off for us in improving student achievement? Are our functions supporting our goals for improving student results? We should look to improve these facets of the school district and align them with our goals for student achievement. Our bottom line is still student achievement.

HOW CAN SCHOOL BOARDS TAKE THE LEAD IN SHAPING THE DIRECTION OF PUBLIC SCHOOL ACCOUNTABILITY IN THE INFORMATION AGE?

Keep it simple. Get started using the data you have available to you even if it is not everything you want it to be. Almost all districts, large or small, gather basic data, such as enrollment, attendance, graduation, and test scores. This is not new information in most cases, but how we use this information is changing significantly. Enrollment, for example, is no longer merely a count of the number of students. It also includes keeping track of the nature of the student clientele served by the school. Test scores have become not just a public report for school bragging rights, but rather a bottom-line accounting of school success or failure.

Don't be defensive. Understand that as more and more data is accessible, it is inevitable that there will be results and information that you do not like. In fact, there may well be information that you would really prefer not to know. The problems we don't know about are problems we can't be expected to solve. On the other hand, when we are aware of problems and the public knows about them as well, we are forced to act. As Jim Collins would tell us, we must "confront our brutal facts." Sometimes the actions we need to take are unpopular, but taking action is always preferable to ignoring or excusing negative information.

Don't blame the messenger. How board members react to negative information determines how much and what type of information they will receive in the future. No one welcomes bad news, so it is natural that board members will be unhappy if school and district results are not what they want. But if the board turns on the superintendent and staff, blaming them, demanding immediate answers, and expecting instant solutions, you can be sure that any future bad news will be obscured in some way. The board cannot generate the data; it depends on the staff to provide it. Unless this information exchange is conducted in an open and trusting environment, the organization will not be able to find the necessary solutions and meet the challenges before it. The board that receives data as a means to inform its decisions rather than as a basis for finding fault is on the road to becoming a continuous improvement organization.

Own your decisions. Too often boards let the superintendent and staff make decisions that are the responsibility of the board. The reasons for this can vary, but frequently the lack of good information is at the heart of the matter. In the absence of good information that is easily understood, board members rely on the judgment of the professionals. The staff's professional judgment may be very good, but the board needs evidence well beyond a sense of good will. It is important that board members seek facts and data to guide their decision-making. The school board serves as a model for the entire district. Board decisions that are founded on the transparent gathering and analysis of information reinforce that same practice by the staff.

Everyone owns accountability for student achievement. Responsibility for learning goes from the board and superintendent all the way to, and including, students and parents. The school board that embraces Information Age technology, and combines it with a focus on using data as a tool to inform decision-making rather than a tool for reward and punishment, is well on its way to building effective accountability. More importantly, the board members are creating an environment in which accountability will serve as the driving force behind improving student achievement.

PROFILE OF LEADERSHIP:
14. CALVERT COUNTY PUBLIC SCHOOLS

Perhaps the most difficult step for a school district is moving from good to great.

Educators in chronically low-performing schools may disagree, but at least in these schools, there are plenty of obvious areas for improvement. As the saying goes, "There's nowhere to go but up." However, in an already high-achieving district, presumably best practices already are in place. Where does such a district find room to improve?

Six years ago, the Calvert County (Md.) Board of Education was asking that very question. Student test scores were at enviable levels at the nearly 18,000-student district in well-to-do southern Maryland. But board members and district officials wanted to do more. The passage of the sweeping federal No Child Left Behind Act, which hold schools responsible for the performance of ethnic and socio-economic subgroups, meant that even the top-performing districts had to reexamine all aspects related to academic performance.

So the Calvert County Public Schools introduced a Student Assessment System, which allows schools to monitor individual student performance. As in other districts that use data to drive academic decision-making, this detailed information is used to guide instruction. Teachers base their lessons on the skills in which the data shows the students are deficient.

The Student Assessment System has students take a regular series of tests, which are closely aligned to the state curriculum. The tests are scored and the results entered into a database, called Clearview, so that the classroom teacher can see exactly which skills are lacking. Teachers then can immediately offer remediation to students who need extra help. The district also redirected a number of teaching positions to address the new priorities.

"It is almost like each child has an individual instruction plan," Ted Haynie, the district's director of system performance, told the *Southern Maryland News*. "While there is much work to be done, the gap in achievement is closing and progress is being made, especially in mathematics."

Superintendent Jack Smith was the district's director of secondary curriculum and instruction when the plan first was introduced and was one of the main proponents of introducing data-driven instruction.

"I used to be a principal and when I was a principal, I would get frustrated by the lack of data," he says. "There was too much lag time in getting the information."

Smith said the school board was supportive of the effort, particularly board members Gail Hoerauf-Bennett and Frank Parrish. Without that board support, he says, the district's plan would not have been successful. With the board's blessing, the district began working with an outside consultant who helped create the assessment and data management program.

According to Smith, a good student assessment program has three elements:

1. It is blameless. Data isn't used to punish principals, teachers, or students. Instead, it is used to assess areas of need and direct resources to those needs. "We've tried to remove the threat of the data," Smith said. "We say, 'How do we make this better?'"

2. It is accurate and immediately available. In Calvert County, teachers can even log into the data system from their home computers.

3. The district's leadership must believe in it. Participation isn't optional—it must be standard operating procedure across the district. "We've made it clear that if you are going to work here, you have to buy into this program," Smith said.

CHAPTER 14

Calvert County's high school gains may be its most impressive, since overall trends show high school students performing at lower levels than elementary school students. Even many districts that have enjoyed tremendous success at the elementary level have had difficulty translating those reforms to high school.

But Calvert County's passing rates on end-of-year standardized tests are at or above 90 percent in the four tested subjects—algebra, biology, 10th grade English, and government and civics. The district's scores are among the four highest in the state for each subject.

The district's academic performance far outpaces that of Maryland as a whole. Ninety-one percent of Calvert County's elementary school students are performing at grade level in reading, compared with around 67 percent across the state. In math, more than 91 percent elementary school students in Calvert County are on grade level, compared with 64 percent in Maryland as a whole.

Similar gaps are found at the middle and high school levels. Calvert County middle school students surpass their Maryland peers by 15 percentage points in reading and 26 percentage points in math. In high school, the Calvert County advantage is a whopping 34 percentage points (86 percent on grade level vs. 52 percent across the state) in reading and nearly 50 percentage points in math (88 percent on grade level vs. 39 percent).

MAKING AYP

Perhaps most impressively, every one of the district's subgroups made federal Adequate Yearly Progress standards. This is true in both reading and mathematics at the elementary, middle, and high school levels. The district doesn't have a single school among its 18 campuses classified by the federal government as in need of improvement under NCLB.

CALVERT COUNTY SEES ACADEMIC GAINS

Since implementing the Student Assessment System, Calvert County's academic performance, which already was noteworthy, has made even more progress.

In 2004, for example, around 73 percent of the district's fifth-graders scored at grade level on the Maryland School Assessment annual standardized test. By 2007, that number had jumped to 90 percent. In eighth-grade math, students gained a whopping 25 percentage points during that four-year span, moving from 47 percent proficient in 2004 to 73 percent proficient in 2007.

In fact, every tested grade level (grades three through eight) saw at least a 5.8 percentage point gain during that time span. And with the exception of third grade, which already was at 85 percent proficient in 2004, every Calvert County grade level posted double-digit percentage point gains in math.

Many districts that have posted exceptional growth have done so by focusing on reading, almost to the exclusion of other subject. But Calvert County has made mathematics a priority, including for struggling students. District officials focus on math at all grade levels and ensure that the math curriculum progresses properly as students move from one grade to the next.

In addition, Calvert County officials encourage collaboration among teachers. Bruce Hutchinson, principal of Calvert Middle School, says his school "makes use of grade-level Professional Learning Communities. With this technique, instructional staff meets regularly to review student data and make instructional decisions. In addition, teachers employ flexible grouping in the classroom, bringing together students who are working on similar skills."

A 2007 report by the Maryland State Department of Education singled out Calvert County's use of data-driven decision making for praise. The report noted the particular gains Calvert County has had in educating limited-English, special needs, and low-income students. Each of these categories consistently has made AYP across the district in recent years.

"The Student Assessment System (SAS) allows teachers and administrators to focus in on various NCLB groups as well as drill-down to the indicator level and assess the needs of individual students and their progress towards various learning. Staff development has been offered to support teachers in utilizing the data obtained from those assessments," the report said.

Recognizing that a child's success in school often is determined by his or her background before starting kindergarten, the Calvert County Public Schools have partnered with a number of local child care agencies to improve early childhood education. District educators meet with day care operators several times a year to discuss what should be taught to preschool youngsters, as well as to share the best methods of teaching young children.

Looking ahead, Calvert County educators say they will continue to work to improve the performance of special education students. While significant gains have been made in this area, these students continue to lag far behind the district as a whole.

The district also faces potential budget cuts in 2009. Maryland funds schools on a per-pupil basis and Calvert County's enrollment had decreased by 300 students this year. Given the state of the economy, it seems doubtful that local sources will completely fill that funding shortfall.

The district also will have to adjust to new leadership as it strives to maintain and improve upon its academic gains. Voters elected three new school board members in 2008, marking the first major shake-up to what had been a veteran, stable board in some time. How these new board members will relate to their colleagues on the board—and how they will steer Calvert County's data-driven instruction plan—remains to be seen.

However, Smith remains committed to using data to improve student instruction. In fact, he is working on a plan to extend this type of data-based decision-making into administrative areas—bus transportation and employee evaluations, for example.

On the academic side, Calvert County plans to look at ways to promote academic rigor and student excellence. Increasing both participation and performance in Advanced Placement courses is one key goal.

"You don't have to be sick to get better," Smith says. "Even really good schools aren't serving all students."

REFERENCES AND RESOURCES

- Barker, Joel Arthur, Ray J. Christensen, Brad W. Neal, and John R. Christensen. *The Power of Vision.* Discovering the future series. [Sydney, N.S.W]: Mind Resources, 2005. (DVD/video)

- Center for Public Education website: www.centerforpubliceducation.org
  A joint initiative of the National School Boards Association and National School Boards Foundation, the Center for Public Education is a national resource for accurate, timely, and credible information about public education and its importance to the well-being of our nation.

- Chrislip, David D., and Carl E. Larson. *Collaborative Leadership: How Citizens and Civic Leaders Can Make a Difference.* An American Leadership Forum Book. San Francisco: Jossey-Bass, 1994.

- Collins, James C. *Good to Great: Why Some Companies Make the Leap—and Others Don't.* New York, NY: HarperBusiness, 2001. (Chapter 2 discusses the concept of Level 5 Leadership)

- Deal, Terrence E., Ted Purinton, and Daria Cook Waetjen. *Making Sense of Social Networks in Schools.* Thousand Oaks, Calif.: Corwin Press, 2009.

- Deming, W. Edwards. *The New Economics: For Industry, Government, Education.* Cambridge, Mass: MIT Press, 2000. W. Edwards Deming's website: www.deming.org

- Follett, Mary Parker, and Pauline Graham. *Mary Parker Follett—Prophet of Management: A Celebration of Writings from the 1920s.* District of Columbia: Beard Books, 2003.

- Harwood, Richard C. "Public Benefit: Entrée or Side Dish?" Article from January 2007. Available on the website of The Harwood Institute for Public Innovation, www.theharwoodinstitute.org.

- National Center for Educational Accountability research on high- and low-performing districts can be found at www.just4kids.org.

- The Partnership for 21st Century Skills website: www.21stcenturyskills.org

- Postman, Neil. *The Disappearance of Childhood.* New York: Delacorte Press, 1982.

- Senge, Peter M. *The Fifth Discipline: The Art and Practice of the Learning Organization.* New York: Doubleday/Currency, 1994. (The Beer Game is discussed on pages 27-54.)

- Senge, Peter M. *The Fifth Discipline Fieldbook: Strategies and Tools for Building a Learning Organization.* New York: Currency, Doubleday, 1994.

- Standards: Links to official state standards and voluntary national standards can be found at www.educationworld.com/standards.

  The Council of Chief State School Officers (www.ccsso.org) compiles information on state content standards

  Achieve, Inc. (www.achieve.org) gathers extensive information on state standards and benchmarks

- Tufte, Edward R. *The Visual Display of Quantitative Information.* Cheshire, Conn: Graphics Press, 2001.

- Wheatley, Margaret J. *Leadership and the New Science: Discovering Order in a Chaotic World.* San Francisco, Calif.: Berrett-Koehler, 2006. Margaret Wheatley's website: www.margaretwheatley.com

ACKNOWLEDGEMENTS

The Key Work of School Boards is a concept developed at the National School Boards Association by a team of NSBA staff and state association leaders, including elected leaders, state executive directors, and other staff. Since the inception of Key Work in 1999, board members and association staff across the country have collaborated to refine its ideas and applications, and several state associations have used it to focus their work in board development for student achievement. The authors of this publication acknowledge gratefully the communal nature of the development of these ideas, and they encourage continued collaboration for their further refinement and application for the benefit of America's children.

This publication was funded in part by a grant from the Microsoft Corporation to the National School Boards Foundation.

The authors thank the many staff members of the National School Boards Association and many state associations who contributed to the creation and improvement of this resource for school board members. We note especially the following:

- Dottie Gray, Manager of Library Services at NSBA, who prepared the "Resources" lists that appear in this book and on the Key Work website (**www.nsba.org/keywork**).

- Kanisha Williams-Jones, NSBA's Director of Education, who coordinated the preparation of the "Profiles of Leadership" chapters in this book and who is responsible for the ongoing resources available on the Key Work website.

- Jeannie (Sis) Henry, executive director of the Georgia School Boards Association, and Ellen Henderson, South Carolina School Boards Association, who developed the "Roles of Board Members and Superintendents" included in this book. This work is excerpted from of a separate publication by NSBA and the American Association of School Administrators (AASA), *Team Leadership for Student Achievement*.

- Kathleen Vail, Managing Editor of *American School Board Journal*, who edited the text of this publication.

- Carrie Carroll, Production Manager on the Publications Team at NSBA, who directed the layout, design, and publication of this book and oversaw Stephanie Wikberg's design efforts.

ABOUT THE AUTHORS

Katheryn W. Gemberling is an independent educational consultant who works with school boards and school district leadership throughout the country on topics related to improving student achievement. She specializes in training principals and other educators on data-driven decision making to improve student results. Her work with school boards has focused on building a strong information foundation to enable school board members to monitor effectively student achievement progress. She has been instrumental in assisting districts in the development of student information systems that guide them in determining return on investment (ROI) for school district policies and programs. Previously she served for 32 years in Montgomery County (Md.) Public Schools as a teacher, principal, associate superintendent, and deputy superintendent. She earned a bachelor's degree from Ohio Wesleyan and a master's in mathematics from American University. Kathy and her husband live in Silver Spring, Md. They have one son. Kathy can be contacted at **kgember@aol.com**.

Carl W. Smith is the executive director of the Maryland School Boards Association (MABE). In that role, he works closely with boards of education and board members across Maryland, promoting local school governance and the leadership role of boards of education. He has held a variety of leadership roles in public education including teacher, principal, director, associate superintendent with the Montgomery County (Md.) Public Schools, and superintendent of the Brandywine School District in North Wilmington, Del. Before coming to MABE, he was an associate professor of education and coordinator of the Educational Leadership Program at Bridgewater State College in Massachusetts. He earned a bachelor's degree in education from Rhode Island College and a master's in history and a Ph.D. in educational administration from the University of Maryland, College Park. He is passionate about the integral role of local control of education and takes every opportunity to make that case. Carl and his wife live in Columbia, Md. They have three adult children and six grandchildren. Carl can be contacted at **csmith@mabe.org**.

Joseph S. Villani is the deputy executive director of the National School Boards Association (NSBA). His responsibilities include coordinating the work of the NSBA staff and working directly with the NSBA Board of Directors and the executive directors of the State Associations that make up NSBA's membership. He previously served for 26 years in Montgomery County (Md.) Public Schools as a teacher, principal, director, and associate superintendent. He earned a bachelor's degree from St. Vincent College, a master's degree from the University of Pittsburgh, and a Ph.D. in human development from the University of Maryland. Joe and his wife live in Germantown, Md. They have three adult children and two grandchildren. Joe can be contacted at **jvillani@nsba.org**.

Bruce Buchanan has been covering K-12 education as a journalist for more than 12 years. During this time, he has written dozens of newspaper and magazine articles on public school reform. He is a frequent contributor to *American School Board Journal* magazine and is the author of the book *Turnover at the Top: Superintendent Vacancies and the Urban School*. He has a bachelor's degree from Wake Forest University and a master's degree in English literature from the University of South Carolina. Contact Bruce at **brucebuc@bellsouth.net**.

ABOUT NSBA...

The National School Boards Association is a not-for-profit organization representing state associations of school boards and their member districts across the United States. Its mission is to foster excellence and equity in public education through school board leadership. NSBA achieves that mission by representing the school board perspective before federal government agencies and with national organizations that affect education, and by providing vital information and services to state associations of school boards and local school boards.

NSBA advocates local school boards as the ultimate expression of grassroots democracy. NSBA supports the capacity of each school board—acting on behalf of and in close concert with the people of its community—to envision the future of education in its community, to establish a structure and environment that allow all students to reach their maximum potential, to provide accountability to the community on performance in the schools, and to serve as the key community advocate for children and youth and their public schools.

Founded in 1940, NSBA represents its State Association members and their 95,000 local school board members, virtually all of whom are elected. These local officials govern 14,500+ local school districts serving the nation's 50 million public school students.

NSBA policy is determined by a 150-member Delegate Assembly of local school board members. The 25-member Board of Directors translates this policy into action. Programs and services are administered by the NSBA executive director and a 140-person staff. NSBA's office is located in the metropolitan Washington, D.C. area.

National School Boards Association
1680 Duke Street
Alexandria, VA 22314-3493
Phone: 703-838-6722 / Fax: 703-683-7590
Web Address: http://www.nsba.org / E-mail: info@nsba.org
Excellence and Equity in Public Education through School Board Leadership